# Butterflies 0–4

Count the butterflies in each frame. Trace the numbers.

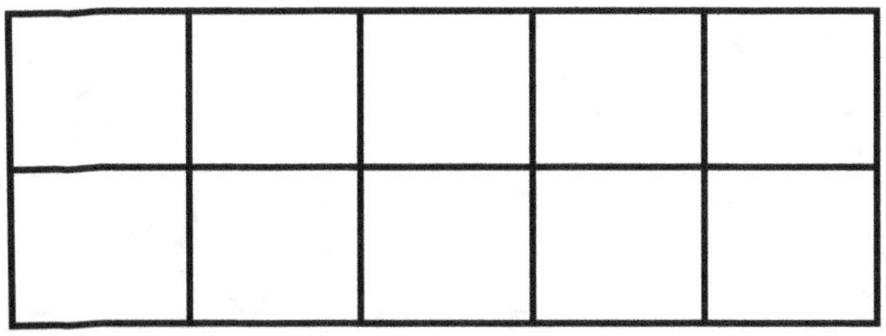

| | |
|---|---|
| (empty ten-frame) | **0**  0  0  0 |
| 1 butterfly | **1**  1  1  1 |
| 2 butterflies | **2**  2  2  2 |
| 3 butterflies | **3**  3  3  3 |
| 4 butterflies | **4**  4  4  4 |

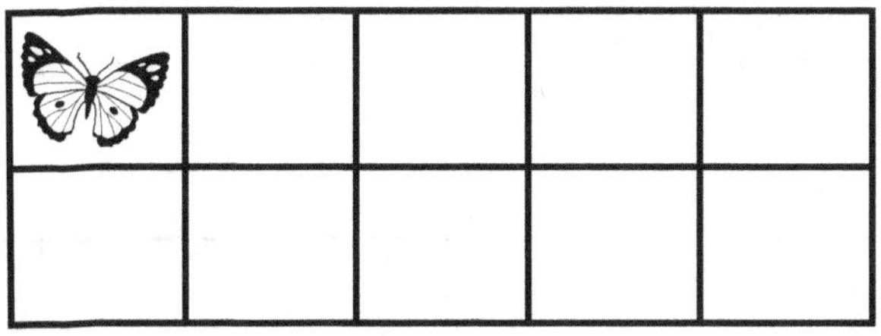

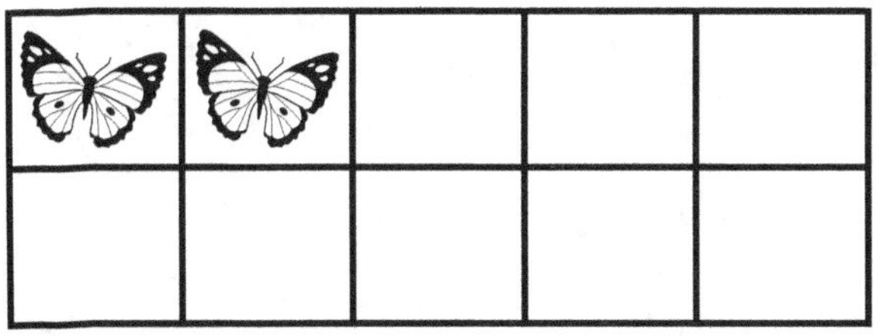

# How Many Dots?

Count the dots on each domino. Trace the numbers.

|  | | | | | |
|---|---|---|---|---|---|
| 0 dots | 0 | 0 | 0 | 0 | 0 |
| 1 dot | 1 | 1 | 1 | 1 | 1 |
| 2 dots | 2 | 2 | 2 | 2 | 2 |
| 3 dots | 3 | 3 | 3 | 3 | 3 |
| 4 dots | 4 | 4 | 4 | 4 | 4 |
| 5 dots | 5 | 5 | 5 | 5 | 5 |

# Find the Match  Sheet 1

Draw a line to match the ten frame to the domino with the same number of dots.
Trace the numbers.

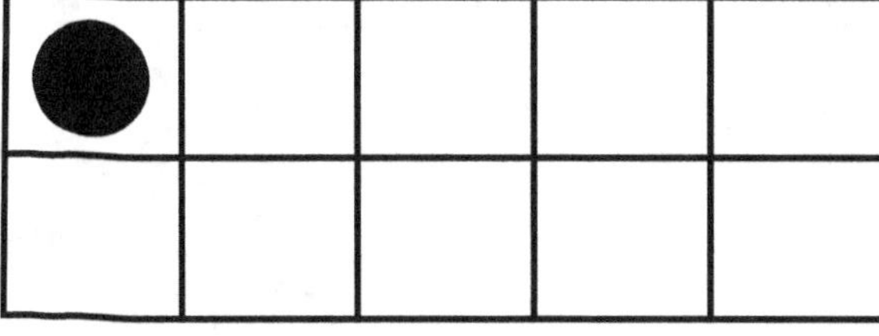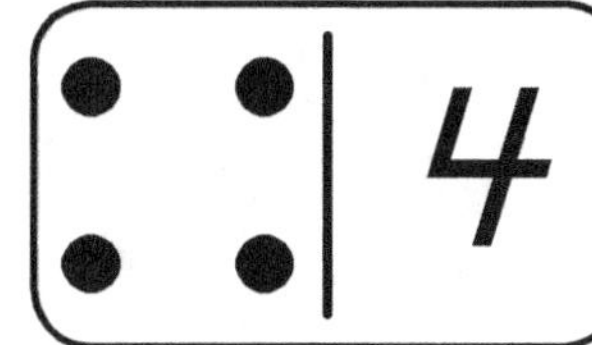

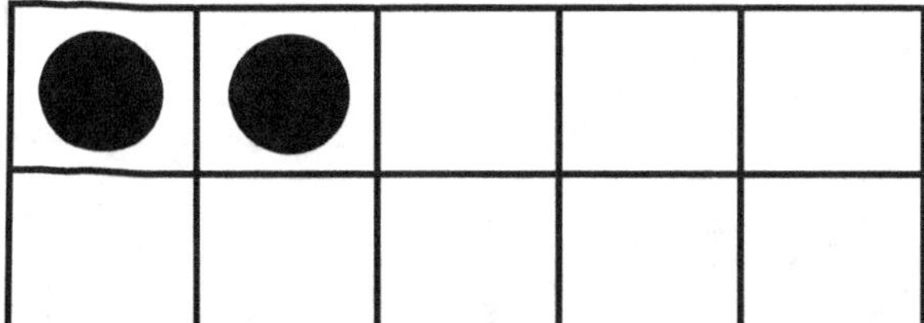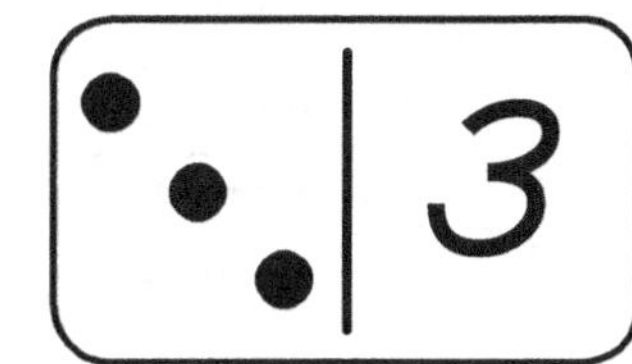

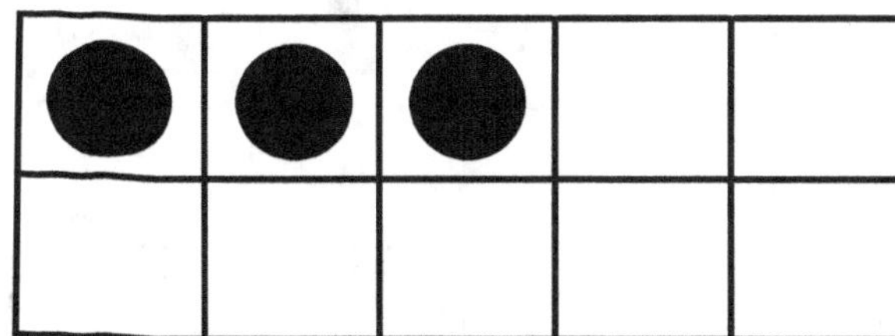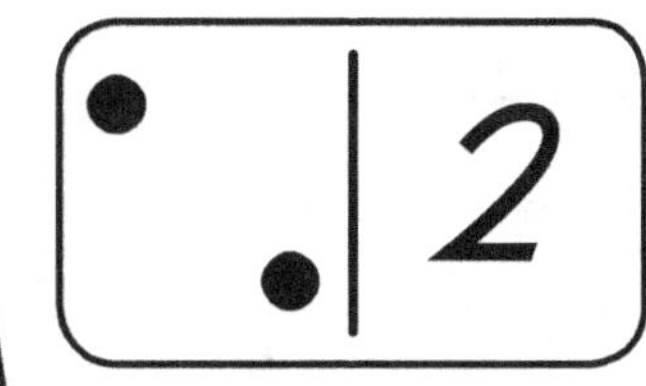

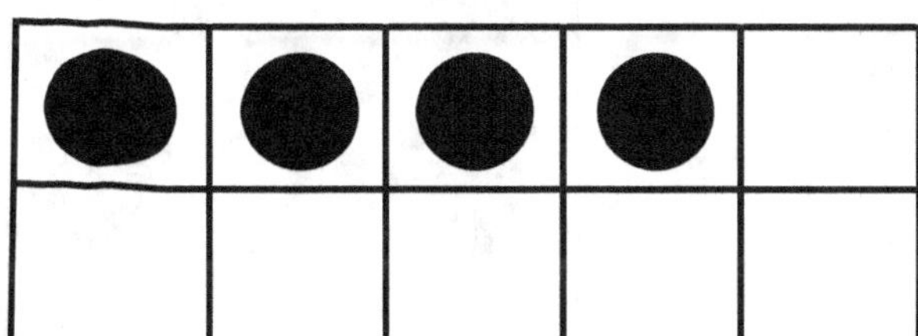

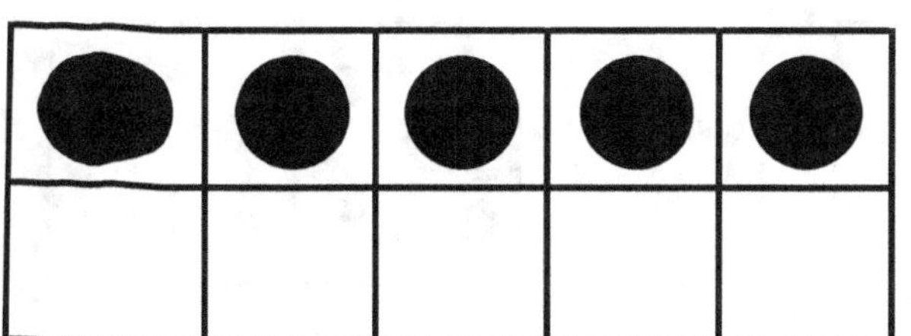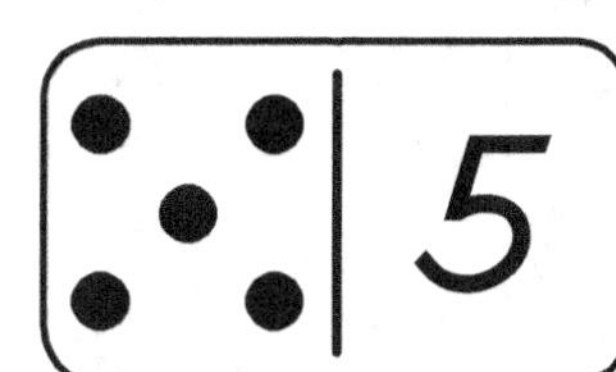

# Bugs in Boxes

Count the bugs in each box. Draw a line to the domino that has the same number.
Trace the numbers.

**1**

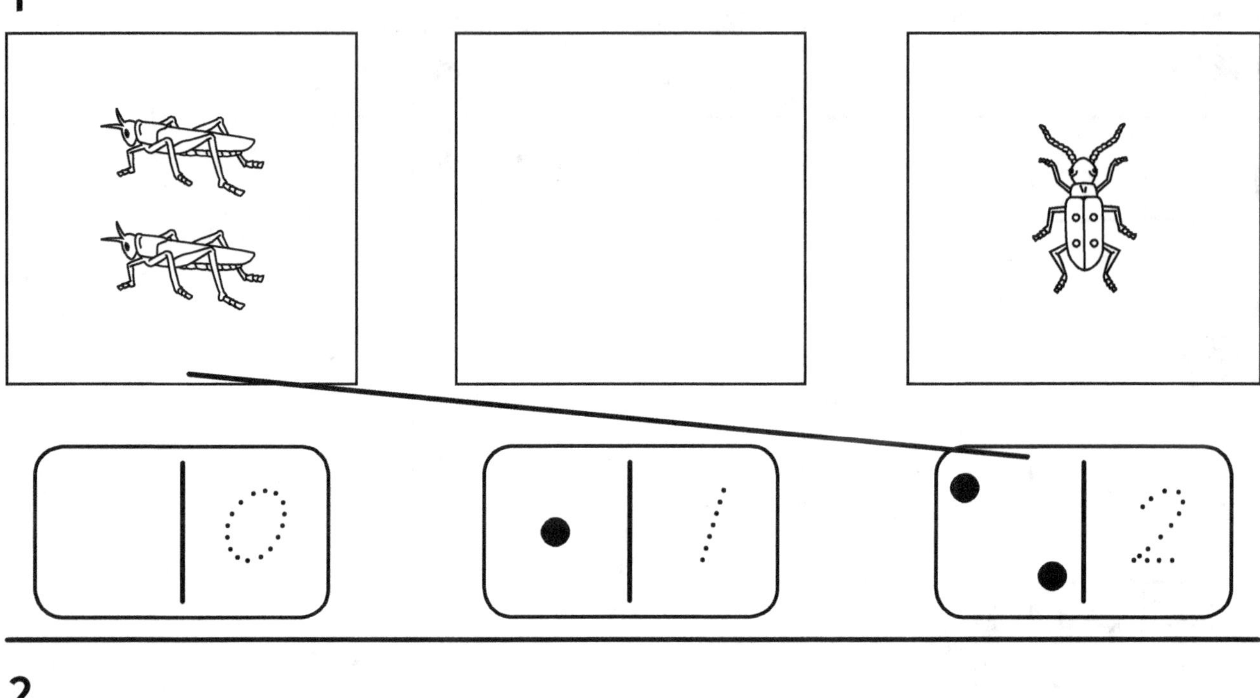

**2**

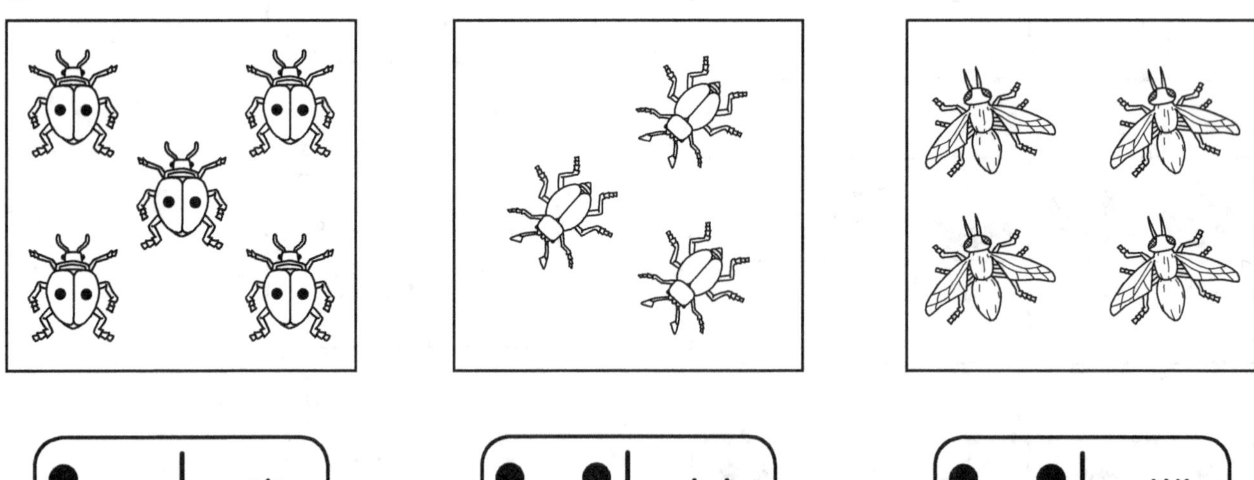

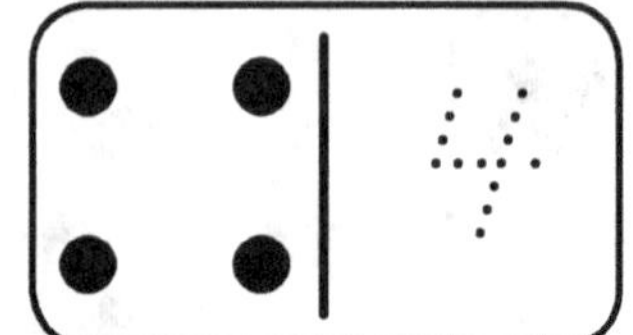

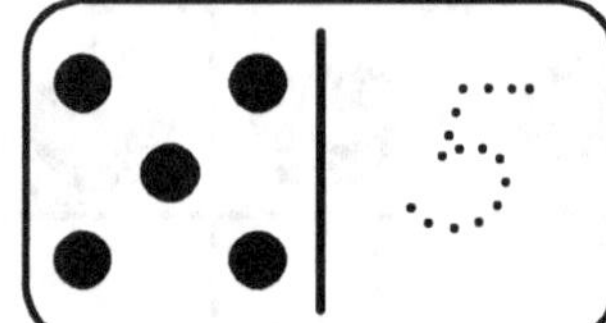

# Sets & Numbers Match

**1** Draw a line to match each set to the number that tells how many. Trace the number three times..

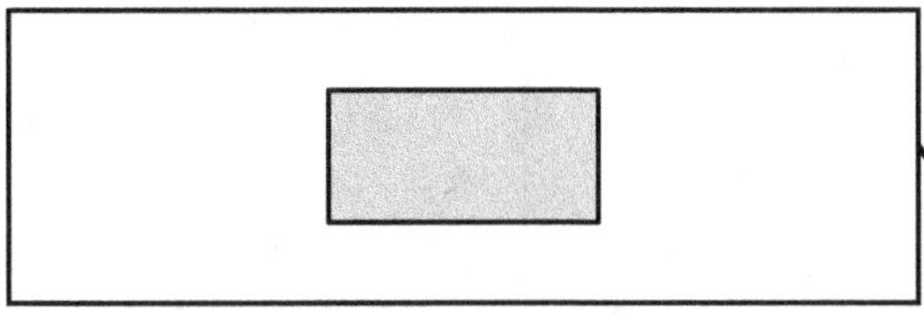

| | |
|---|---|
| | 3 circles<br>3  3  3 |
| 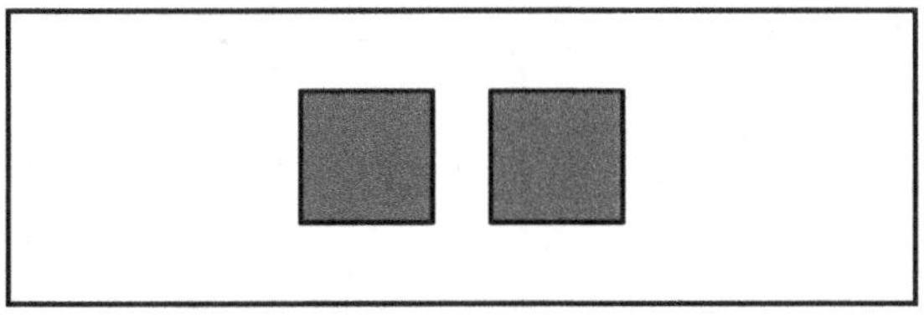 | 1 rectangle<br>1  1  1 |
| 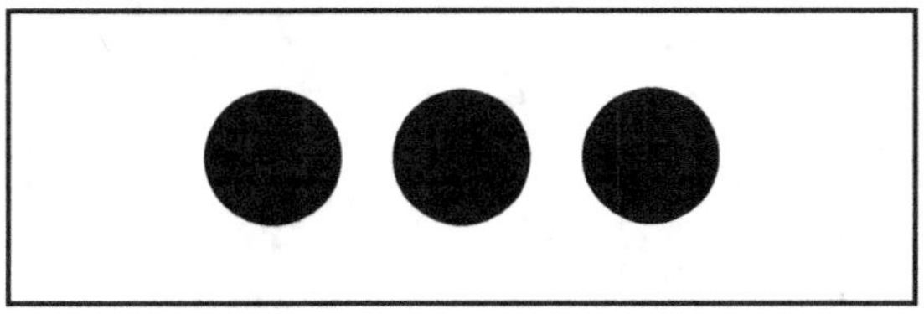 | 4 stars<br>4  4  4 |
| 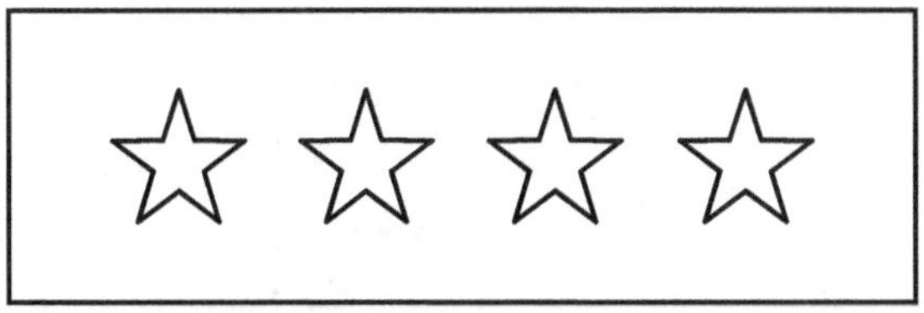 | 2 squares<br>2  2  2 |
| 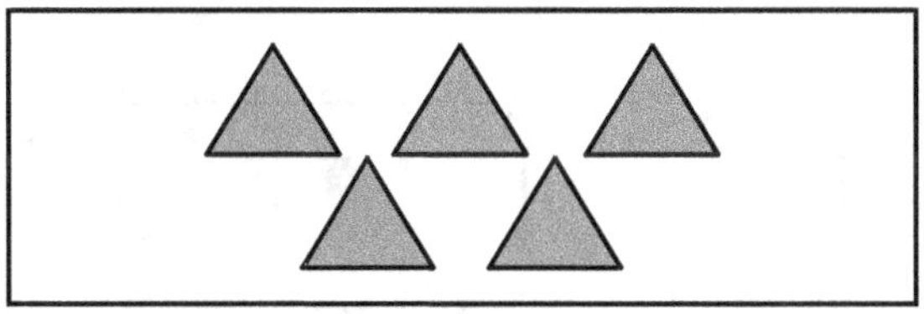 | 5 triangles<br>5  5  5 |

**2** Trace the numbers below.

0   1   2   3   4   5

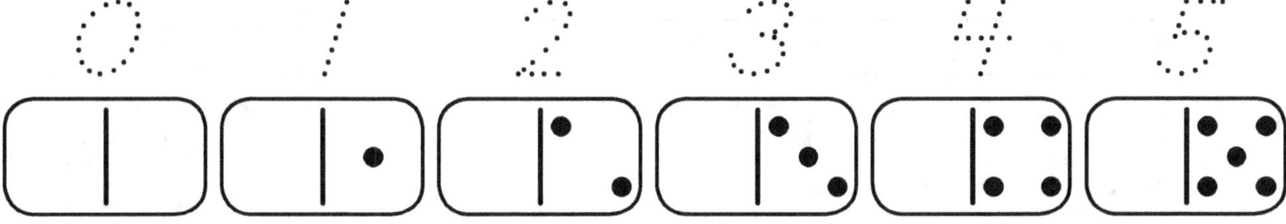

# Counting Cubes

Color the cubes as indicated. Draw a line to the domino that has the same number. Trace the numbers.

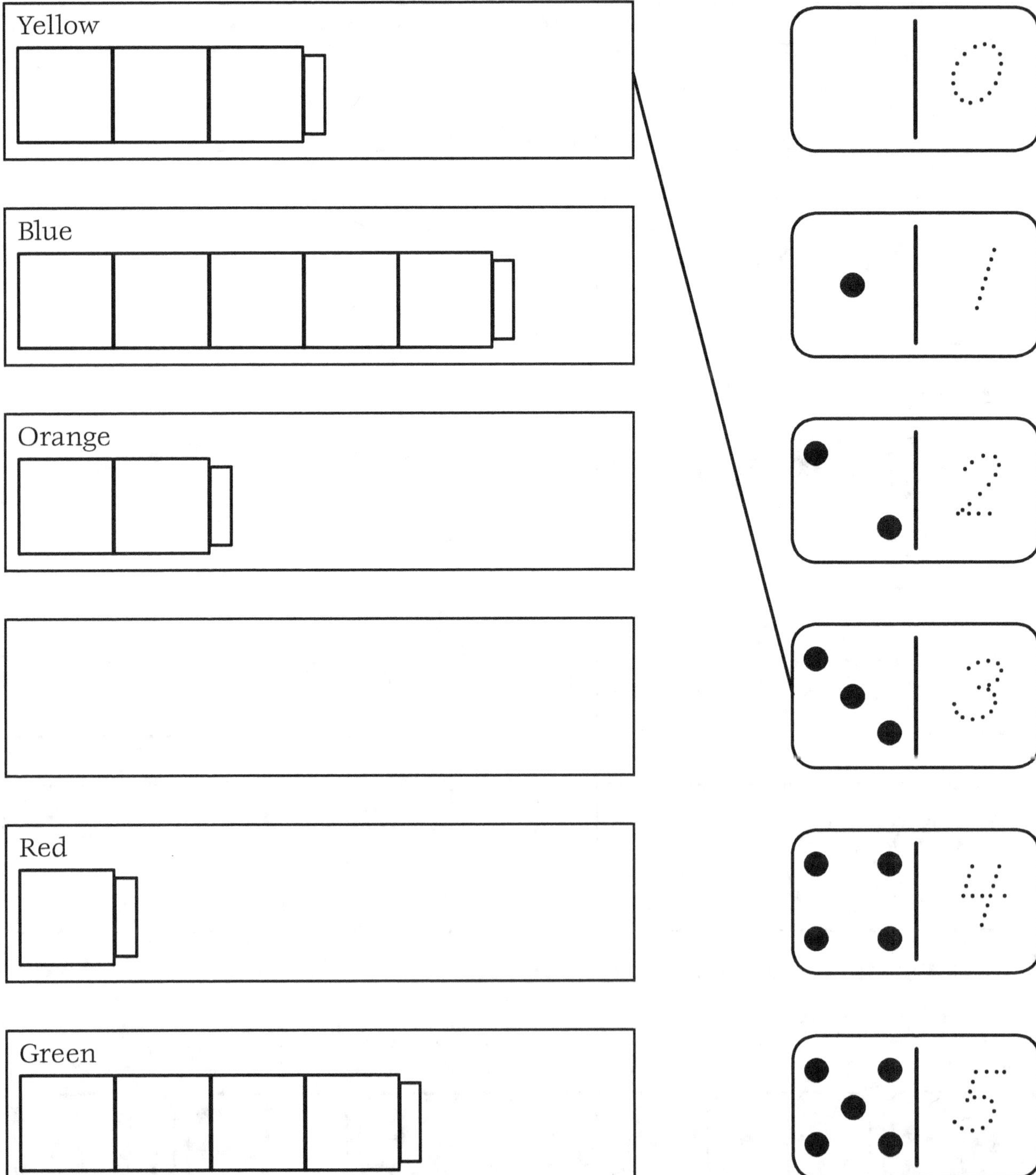

NAME ____________________ DATE ____________

# Shapes & Numbers

**1** Color the number of shapes as indicated below.

Color 5 squares:

Color 4 rectangles:

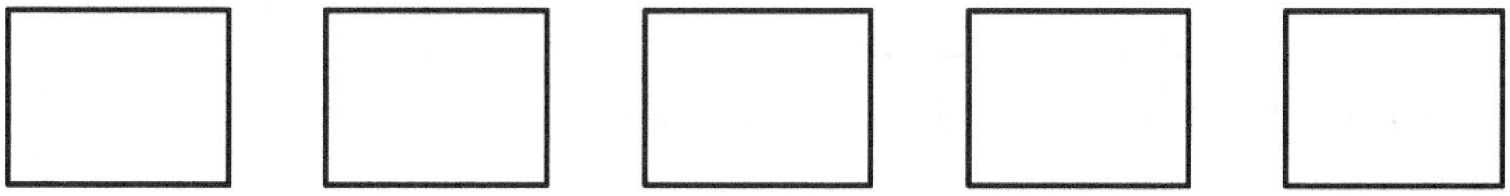

Color 2 triangles:

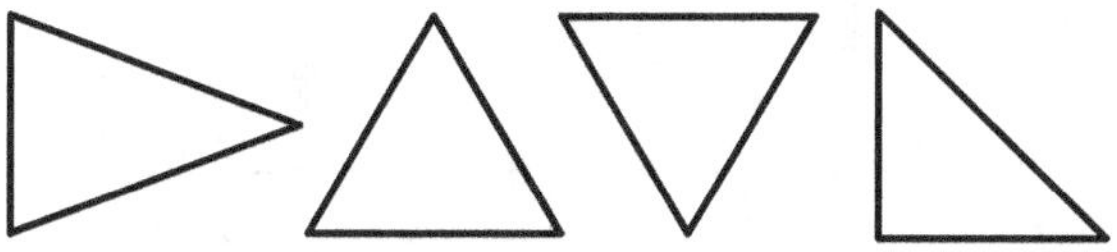

Color 3 circles:

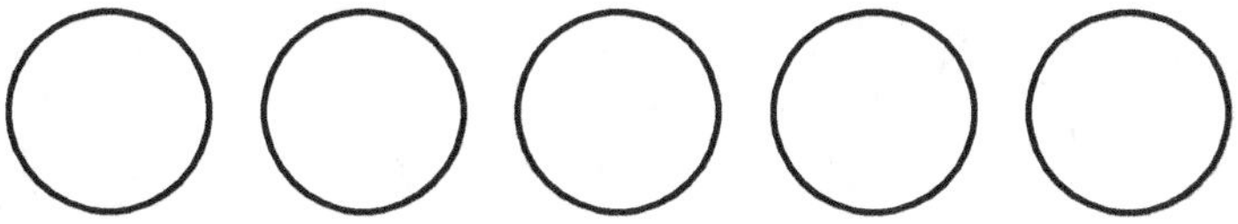

**2** Trace the numbers.

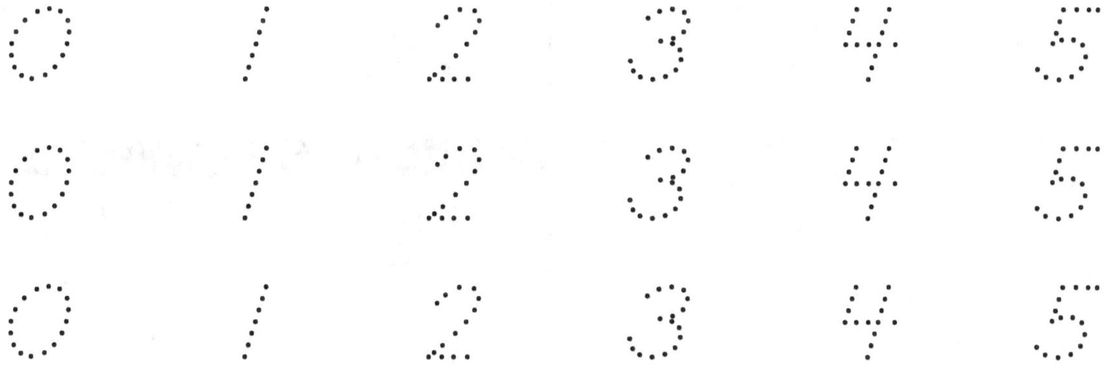

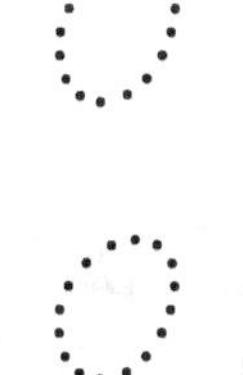

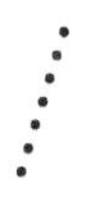

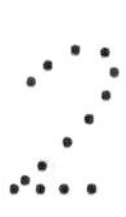

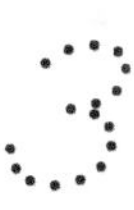

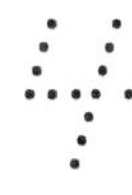

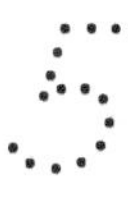

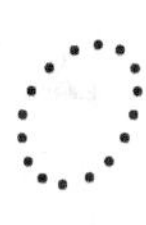

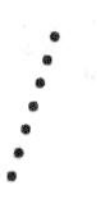

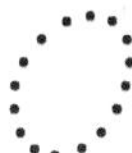

# Triangles, Squares & Rectangles  How Many Sides?

**1** Trace the numbers.

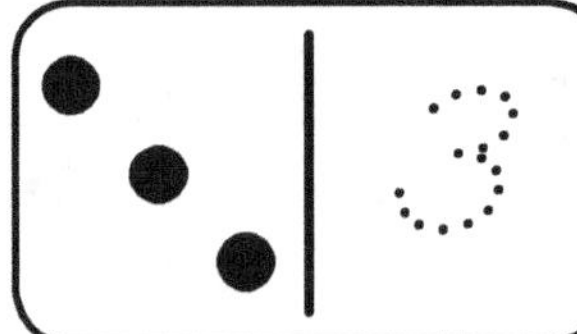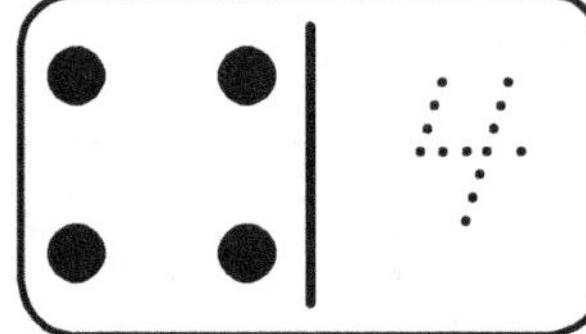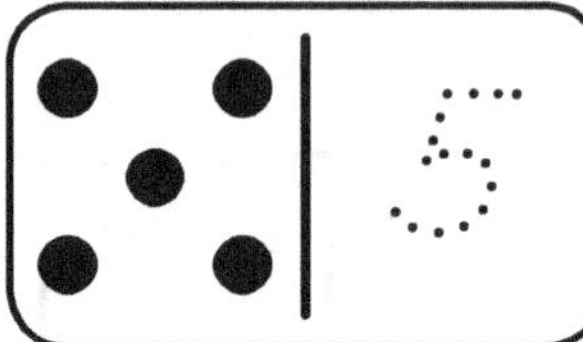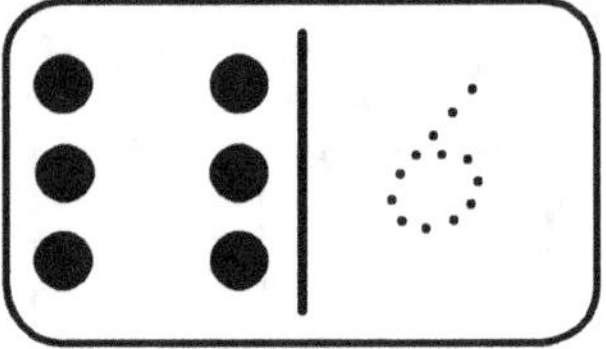

**2** Count and record the number of sides on each shape. You can add an arrow on each side if it helps.

| | |
|---|---|
| Triangle How many sides? | Triangle How many sides? |
| Rectangle How many sides? | Square How many sides? |
| Triangle How many sides? | Rectangle How many sides? |
| Square How many sides? | **CHALLENGE**<br>Hexagon How many sides? |

# Triangles, Squares & Rectangles  How Many Corners?



**1** Trace the numbers.

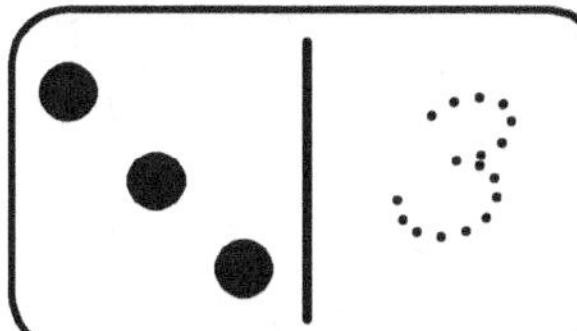 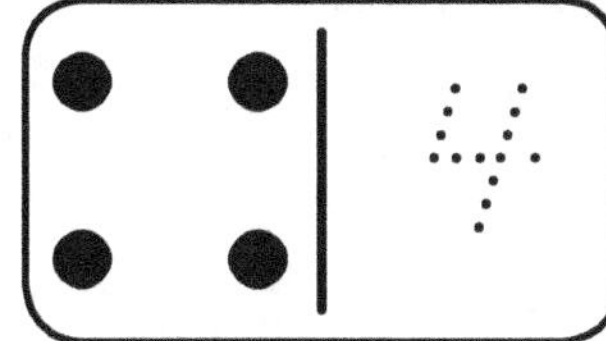 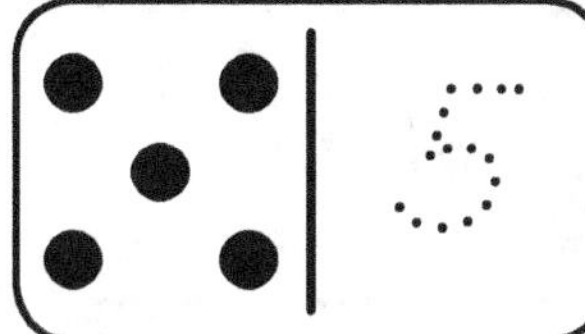 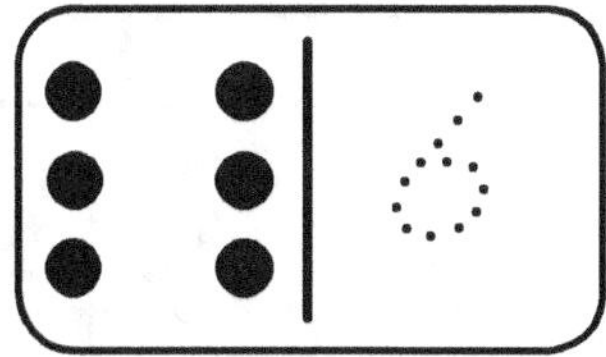

**2** Count and record the number of corners on each shape. You can add an arrow at each corner if it helps.

| | |
|---|---|
| Triangle    How many corners? | Triangle    How many corners? |
| Rectangle    How many corners? | Square    How many corners? |
| Triangle    How many corners? | Rectangle    How many corners? |
| Square    How many corners? | **CHALLENGE**<br>Hexagon    How many corners? |

# Ladybugs 5–9

Count the ladybugs in each frame. Trace the numbers.

# More Dots

Count the dots on each domino. Trace the numbers.

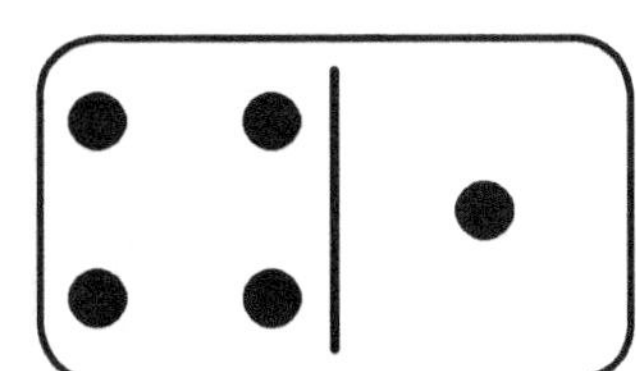 **5**  5 5 5 5

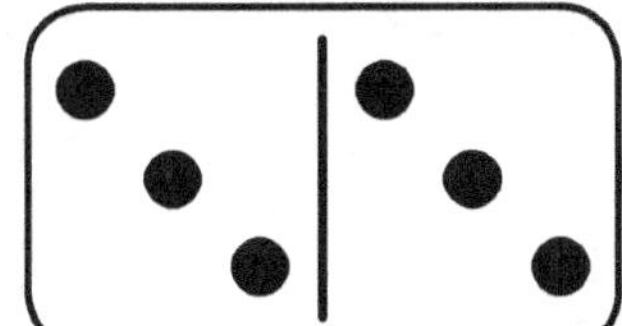 **6**  6 6 6 6

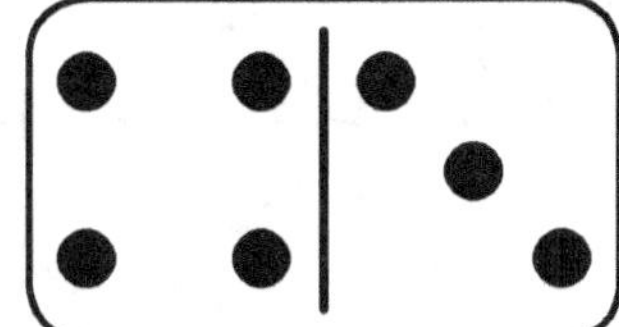 **7** 7 7 7 7

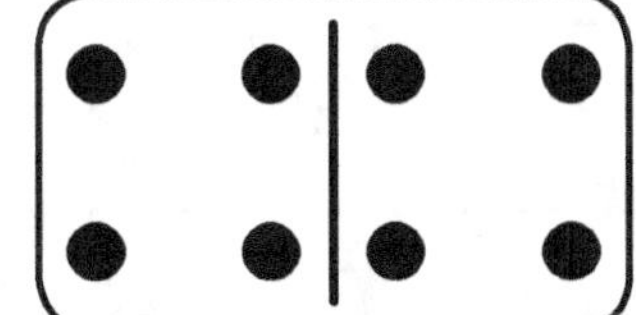 **8**  8 8 8 8

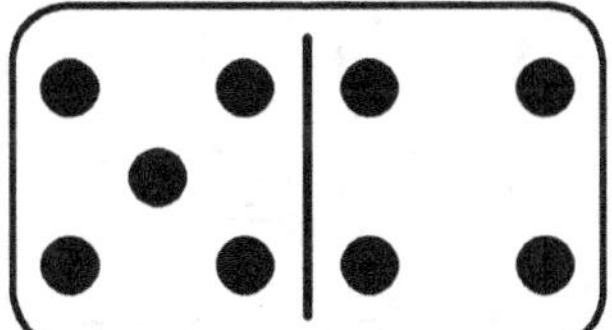 **9**  9 9 9 9

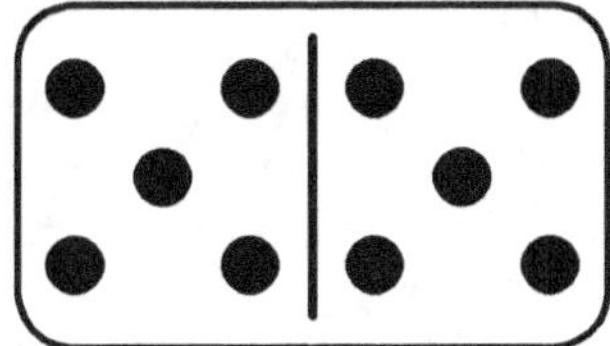 **10**  10 10 10 10

# Shape Patterns

Draw the 3 shapes you think should come next in each pattern below.

**1**

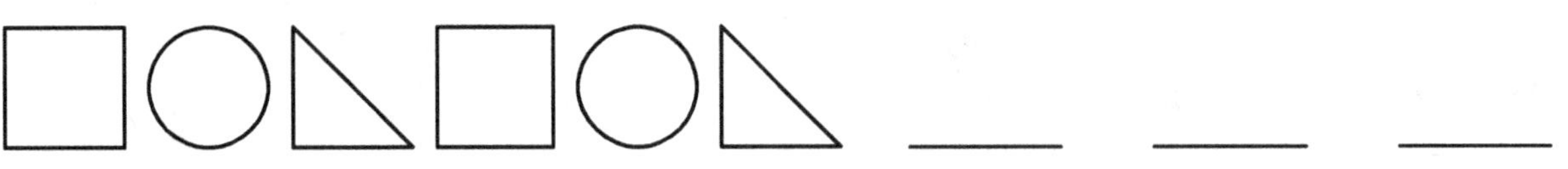

**2**

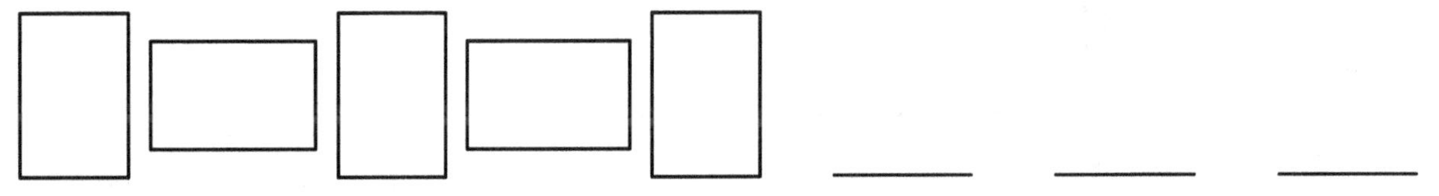

**3**

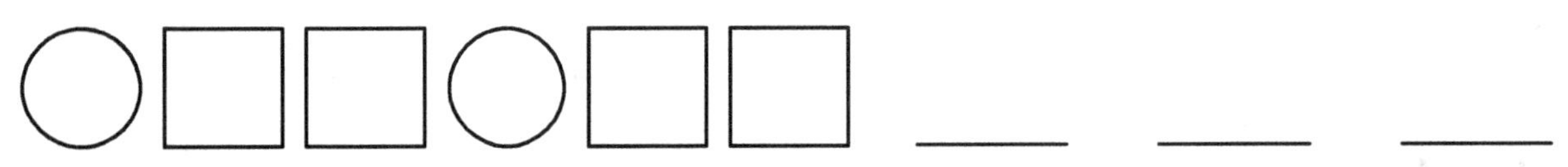

**4**

**5**

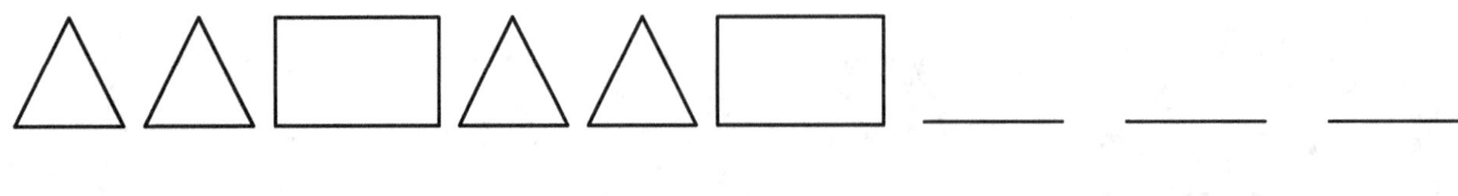

# Find the Match  Sheet 2

Draw a line to match the ten frame to the domino with the same number of dots.
Trace the numbers.

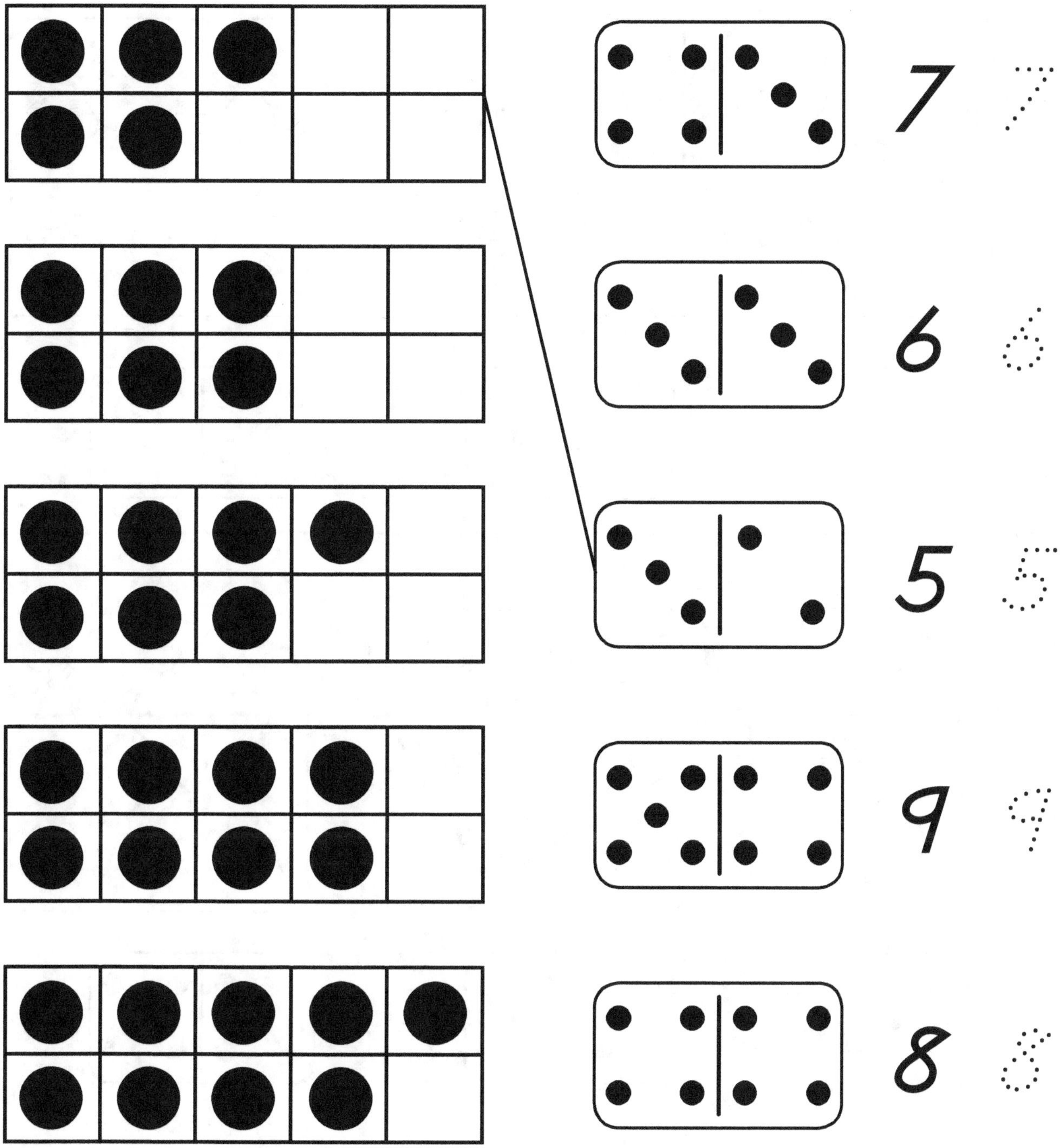

7   7

6   6

5   5

9   9

8   8

# More Bugs in Boxes

Count the bugs in each box. Draw a line to the domino that has the same number. Trace the numbers.

**1**

 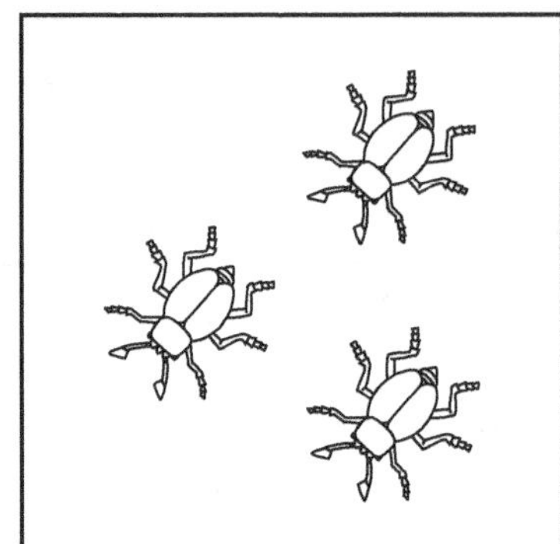 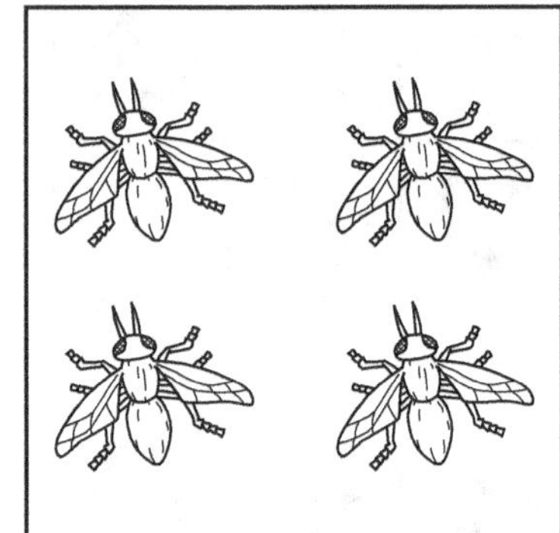

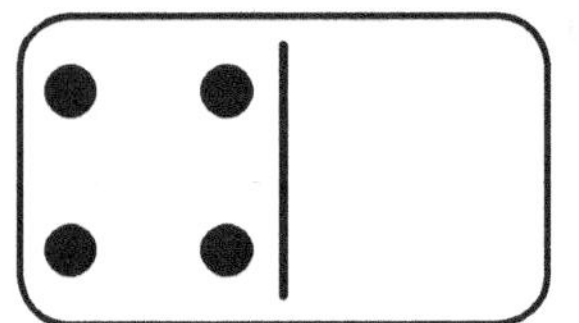  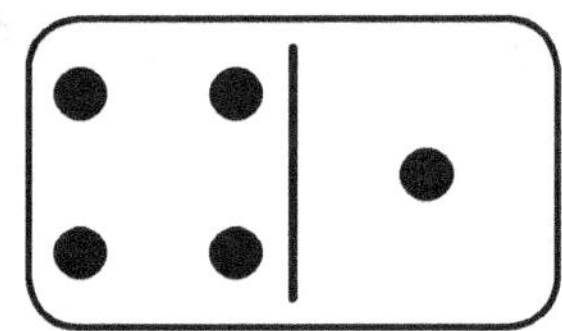  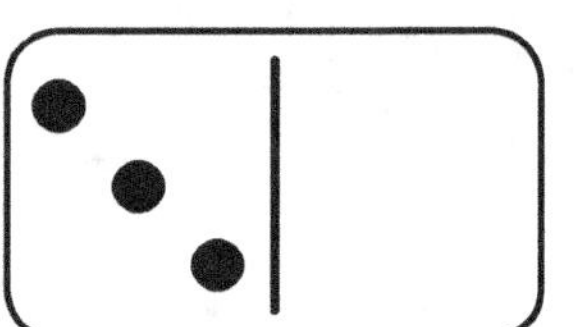

---

**2**

  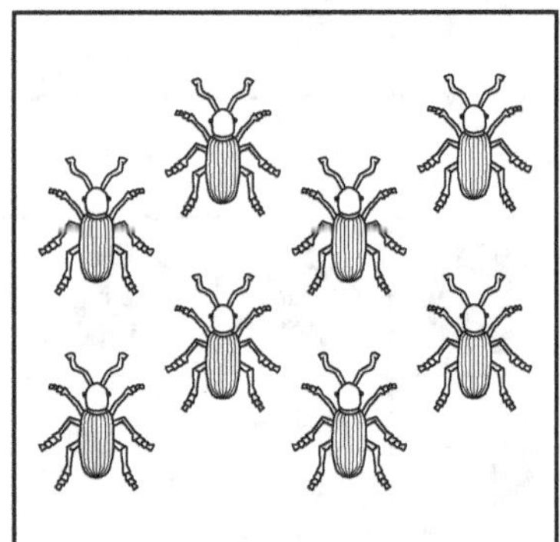

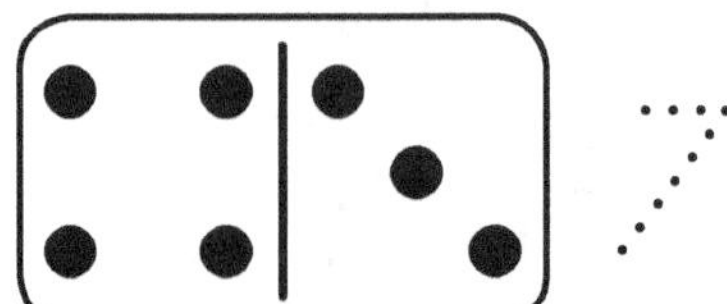 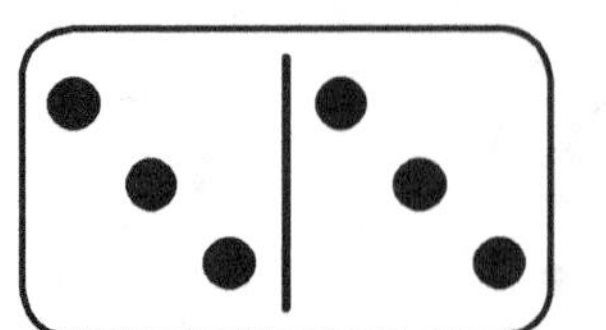 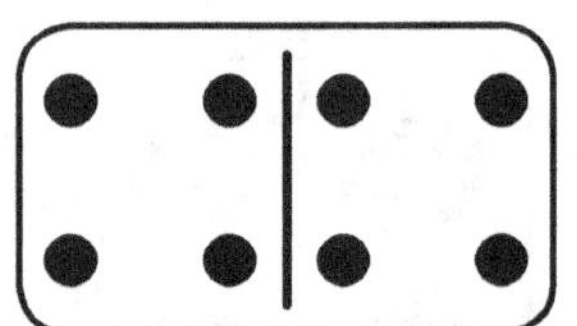

# Fill the Boxes



**1** Trace the numbers.

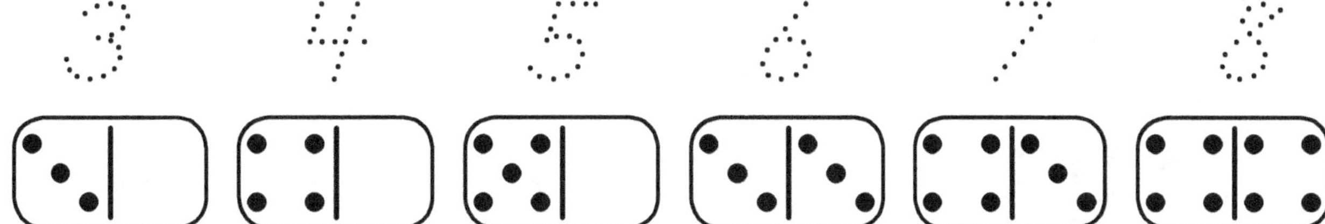

**2** Draw the items below.

| | |
|---|---|
| Draw 3 bugs. | |
| Draw 4 dots. | |
| Draw 5 lines. | |
| Draw 6 eggs. | |
| Draw 7 hearts. | |

NAME ______________________ DATE ____________

# Dot-to-Dot

**1** Trace the numbers. Draw a line from each number to the matching domino.

1 2 3 4 5 6 7 8 9

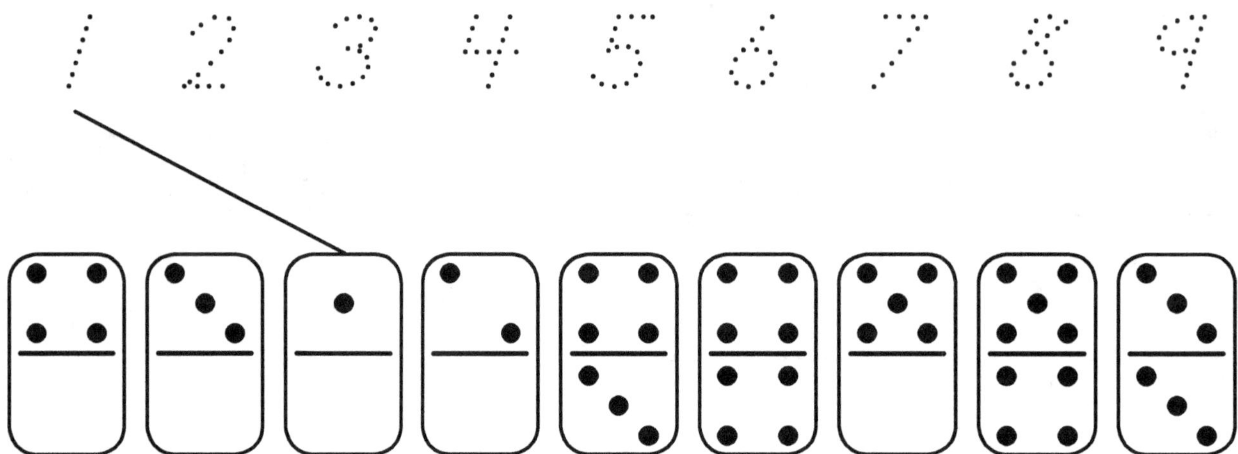

**2** Trace the numbers. Connect the dots in order to make a picture.

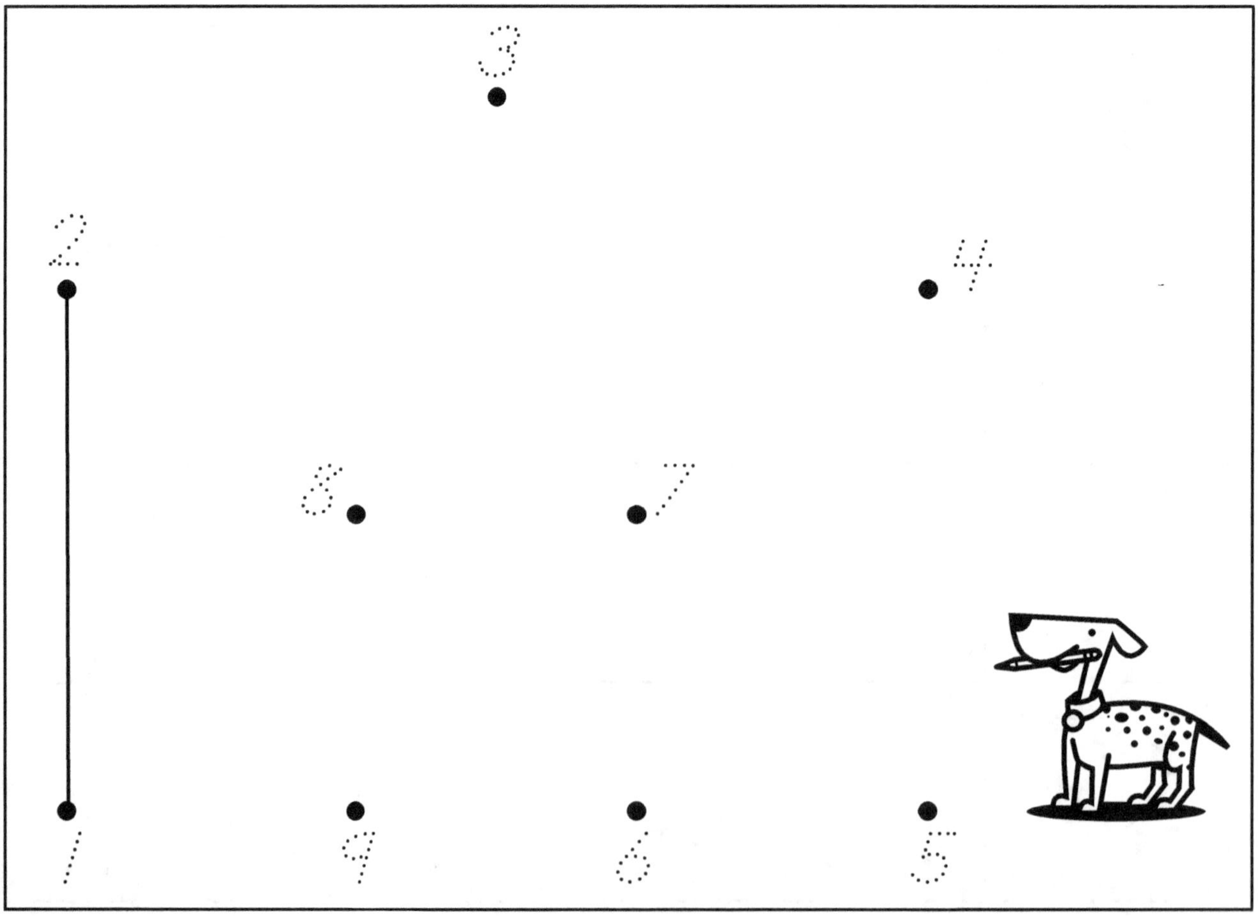

# Patterns  What Comes Next?

**1** Draw or color what you think comes next in the pattern.

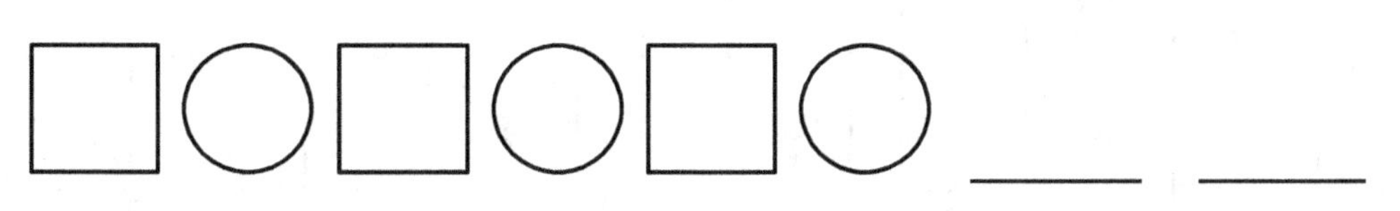

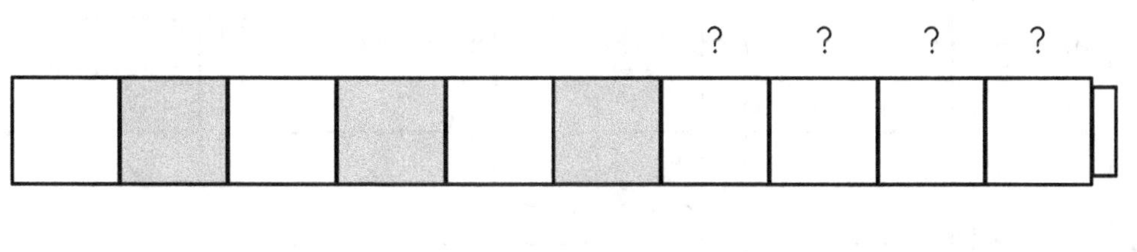

**2** Fill in the numbers that are missing.

1  ____  3  4  5  ____  7  8  ____  10

NAME ______________________________ DATE ______________

# How Many? Sheet 1

Use the numbers and the dominoes to help solve the problems below.

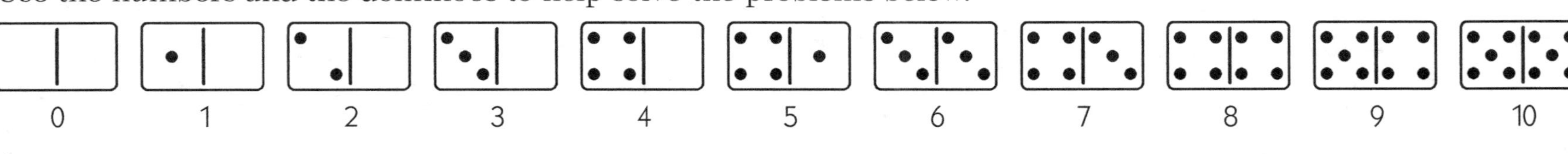

0 1 2 3 4 5 6 7 8 9 10

**1** Count the bugs and record the number.

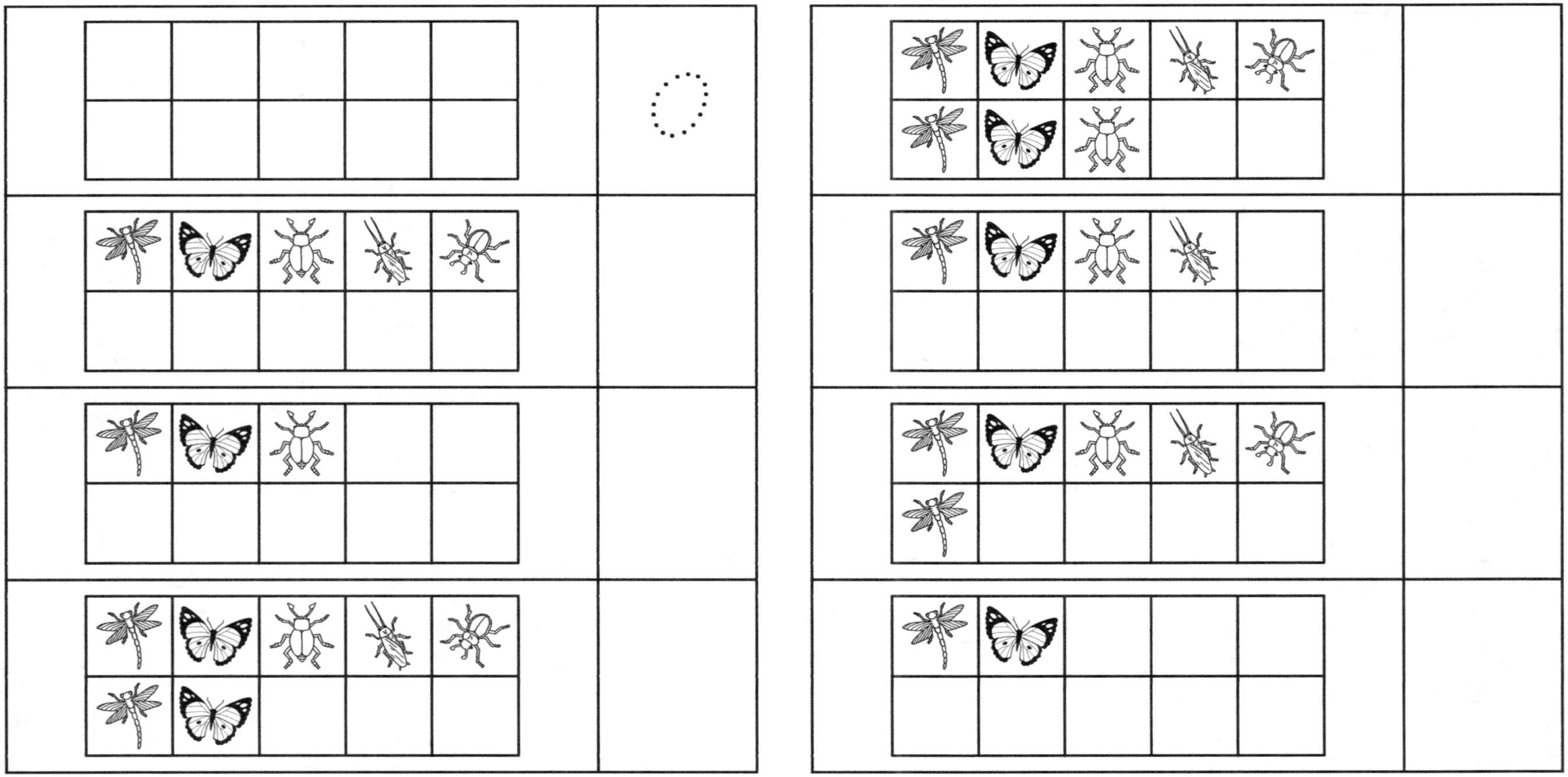

NAME ____________________ DATE ____________

# **Tallying** How Many Sticks?

Use the numbers and dominoes to help solve the problems below.

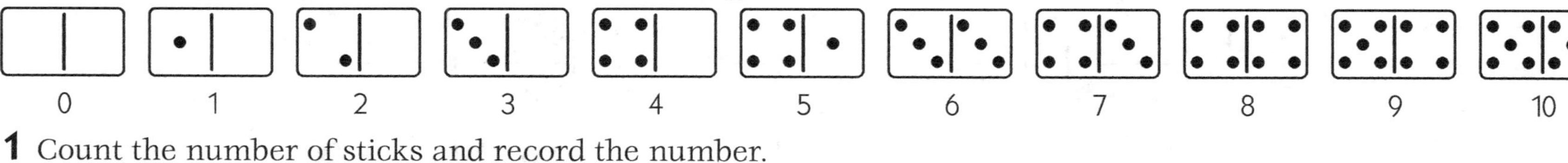

0 1 2 3 4 5 6 7 8 9 10

**1** Count the number of sticks and record the number.

| | | | |
|---|---|---|---|
|  | 3 |  | |
|  | |  | |
|  | |  | |

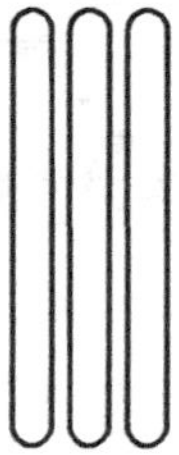

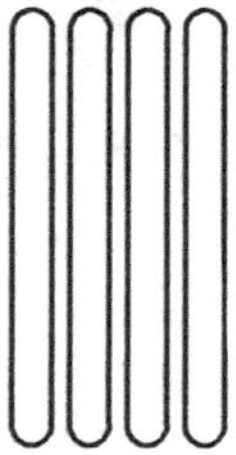

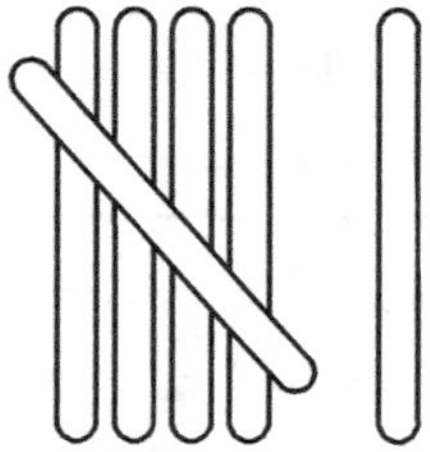

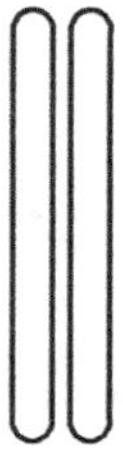

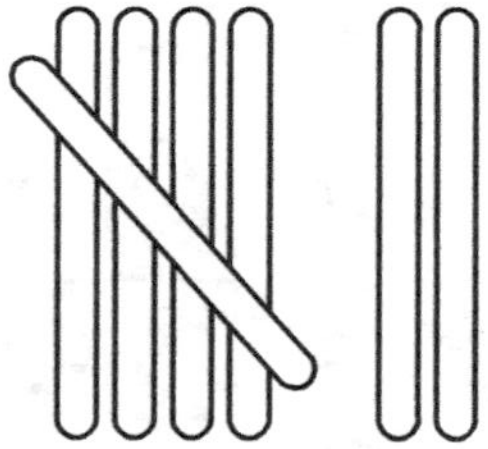

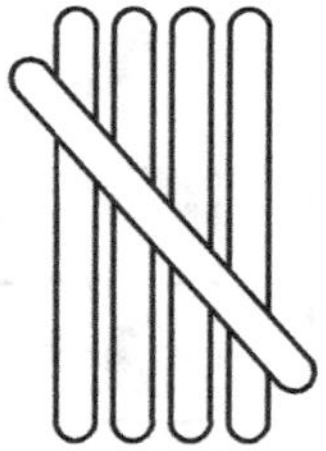

NAME ______________________ DATE ______________

# How Many? Sheet 2

Use the numbers to help solve the problems below.

0 1 2 3 4 5 6 7 8 9 10

Count the number of dots and record the number.

| | | | |
|---|---|---|---|
| 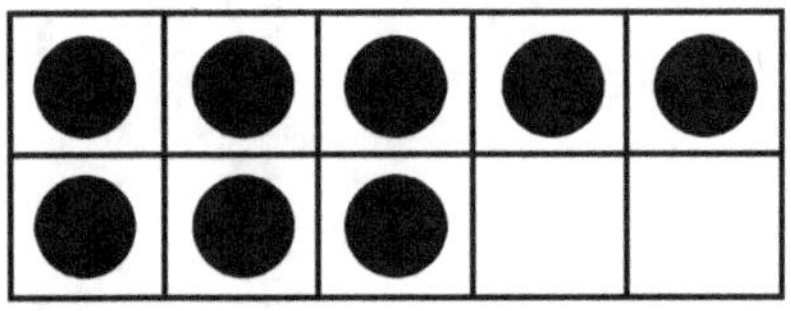 | 8 | 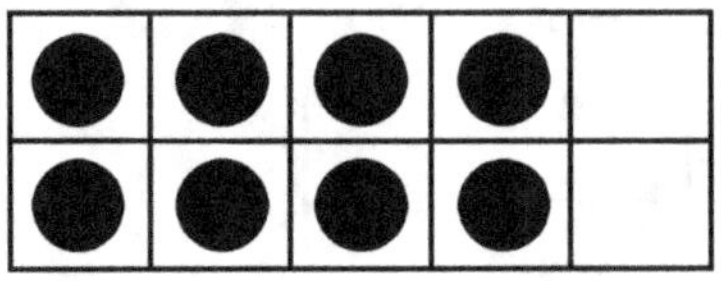 | |
| 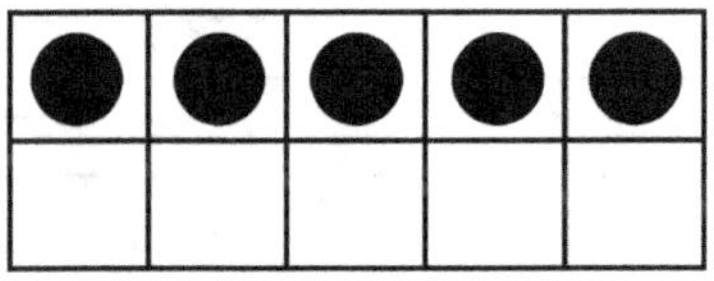 | | 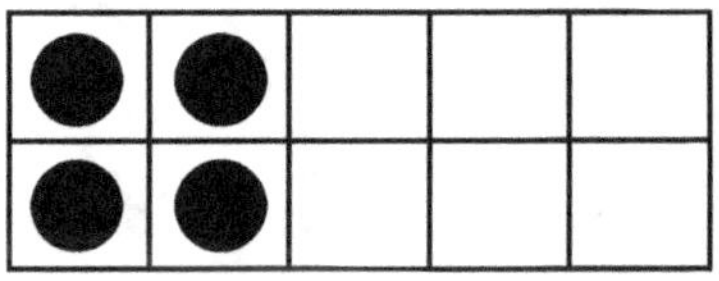 | |
| 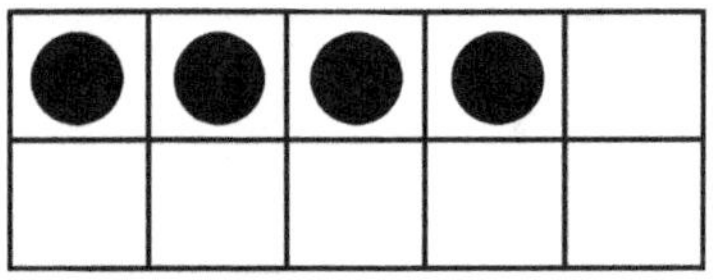 | | 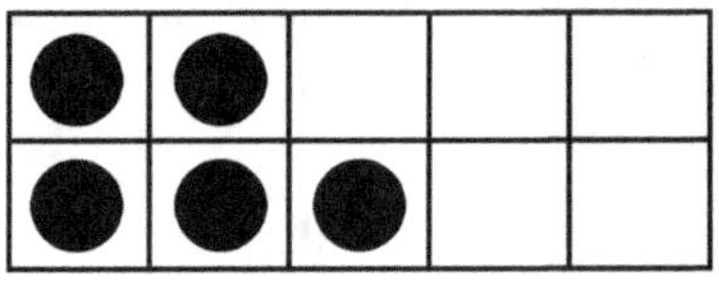 | |
| 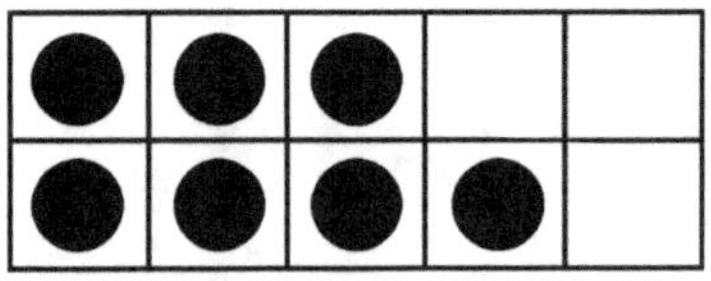 | | 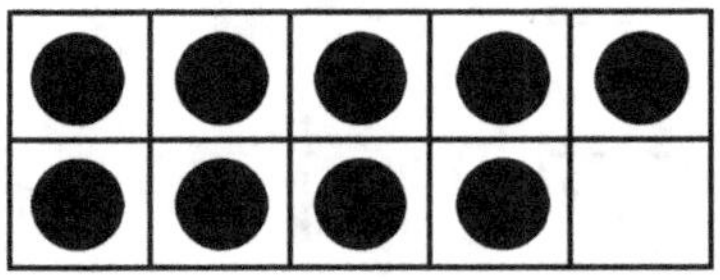 | |
| 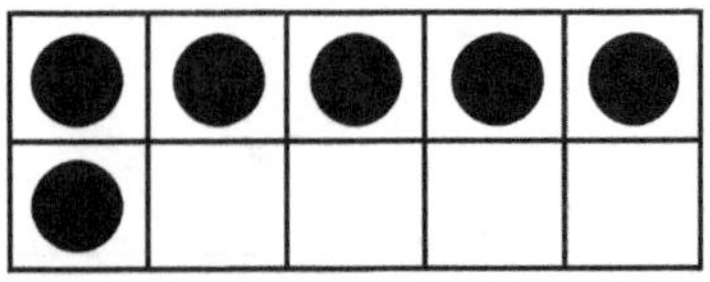 | | 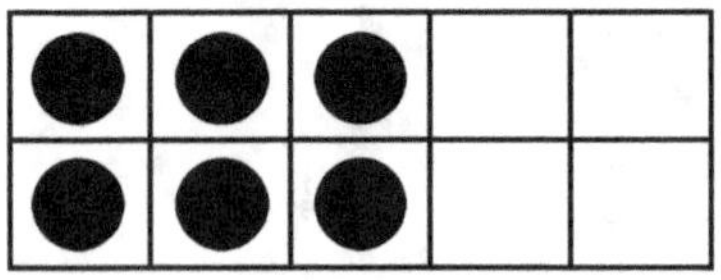 | |
| 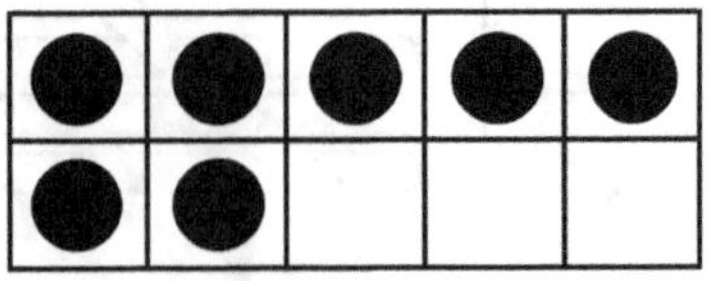 | | 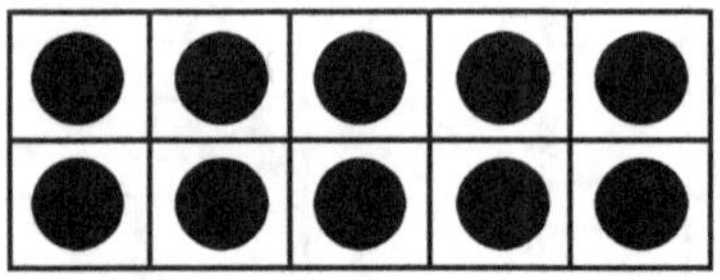 | |

# Can You Find the Match?

Draw a line from the ten frame to the tally sticks that match.

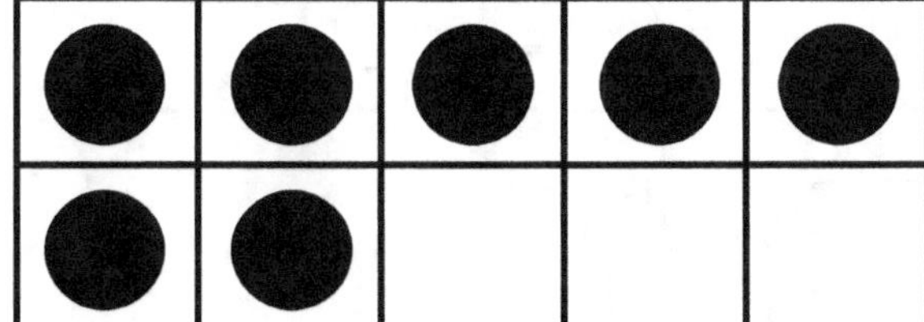

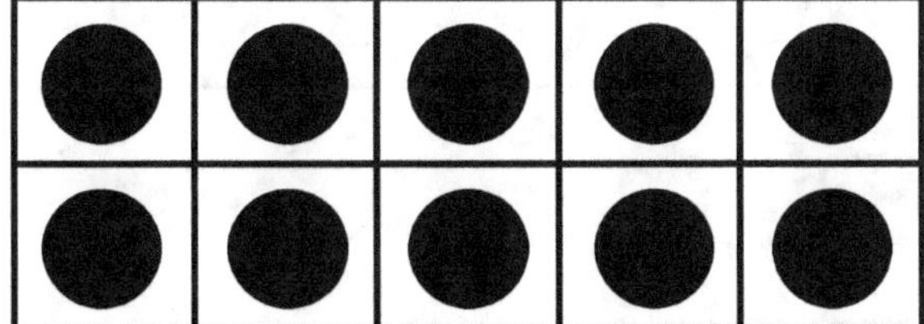

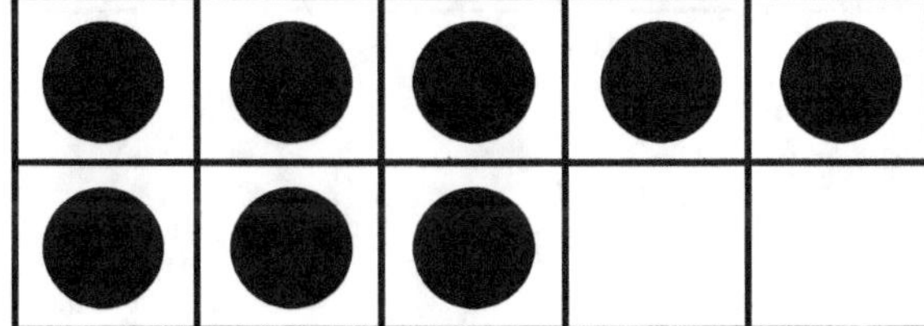

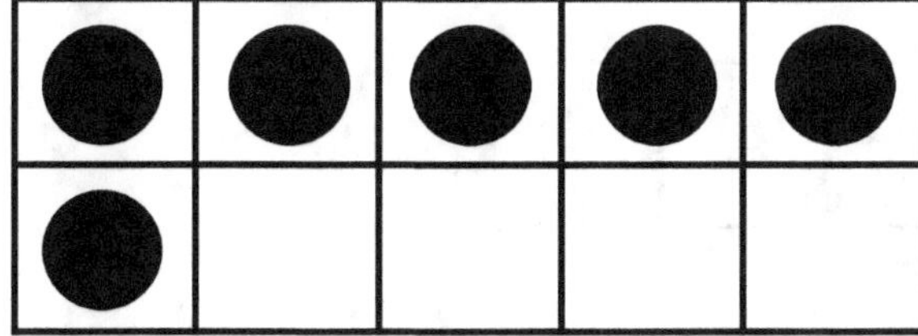

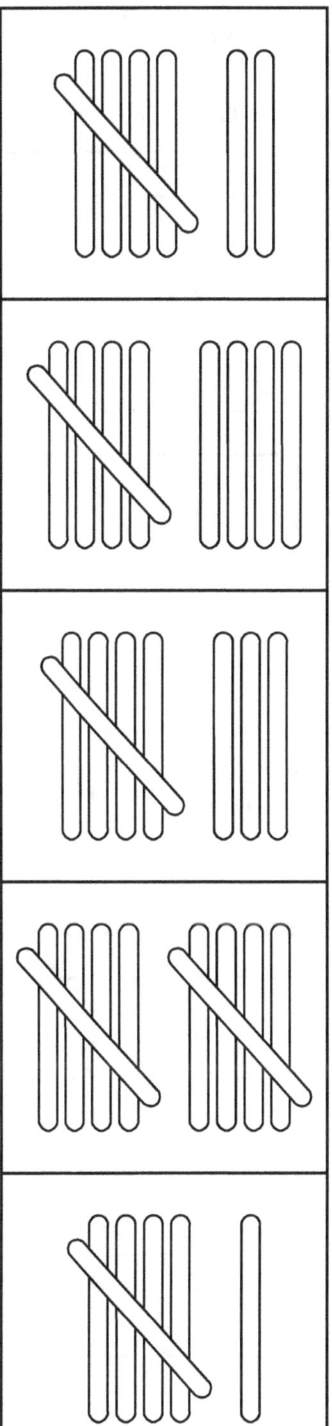

# Adding One More

Use the numbers to help solve the problems below.

0   1   2   3   4   5   6   7   8   9   10

Solve the addition problems. Use the pictures to help.

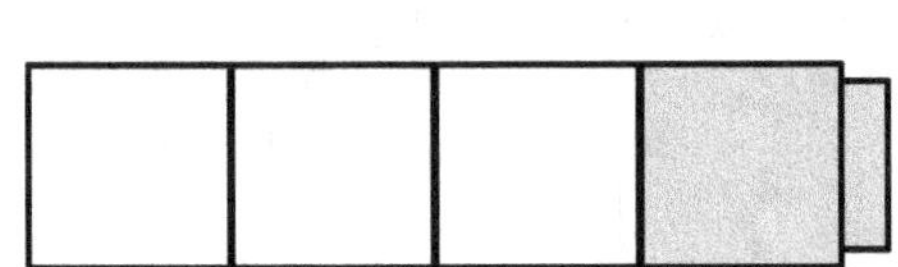

3 + 1 = _______

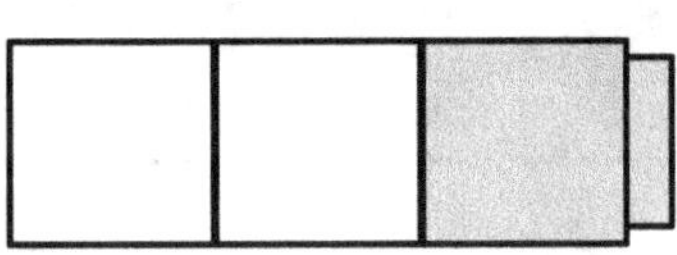

2 + 1 = _______

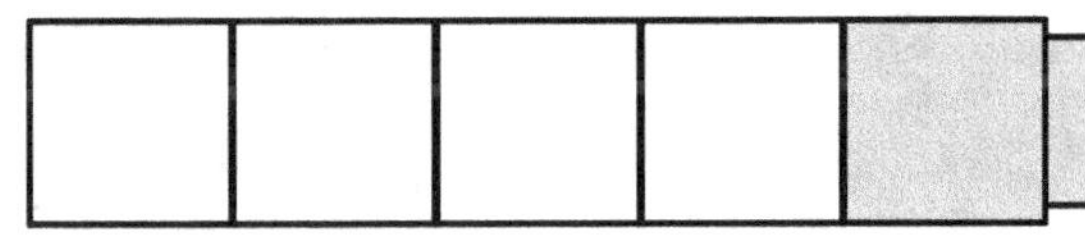

4 + 1 = _______

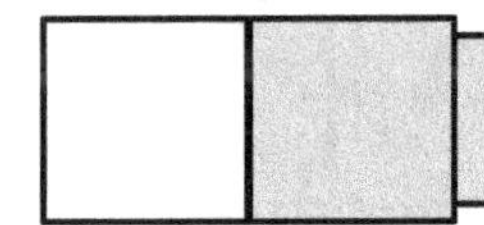

1 + 1 = _______

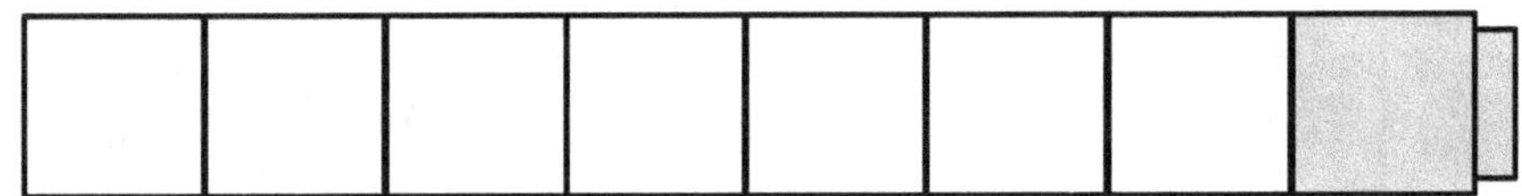

7 + 1 = _______

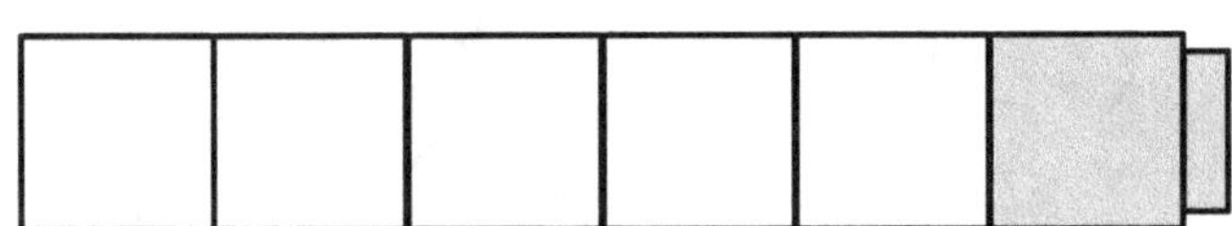

5 + 1 = _______

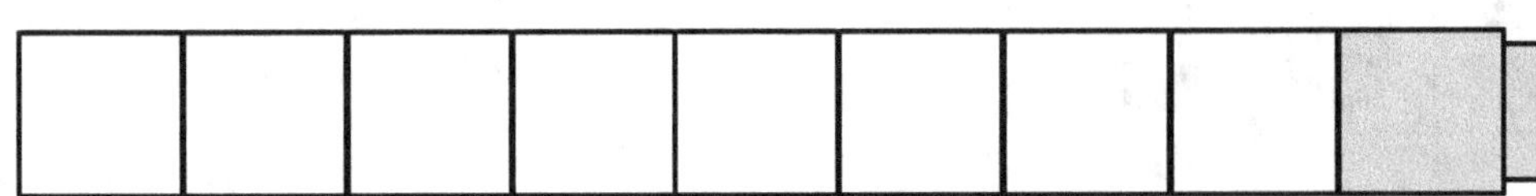

8 + 1 = _______

# Butterfly Countdown Subtract One

Solve the subtraction problems. Use the pictures to help.

10 – 1 = _______

8 – 1 = _______

4 – 1 = _______

6 – 1 = _______

7 – 1 = _______

2 – 1 = _______

# Add a Circle

Trace the numbers and complete the addition problems below. Use the pictures to help.

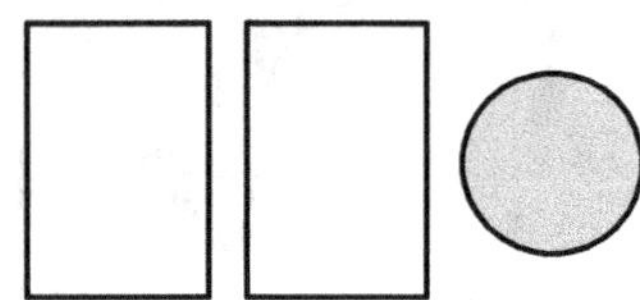

$$2 + 1 = \underline{3}$$

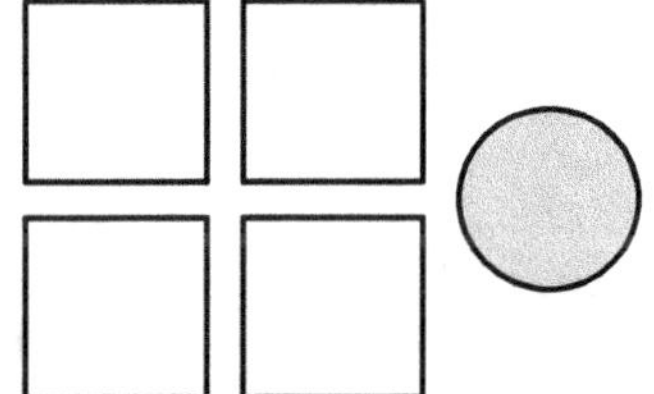

$$4 + 1 = \underline{5}$$

$$6 + 1 = \underline{7}$$

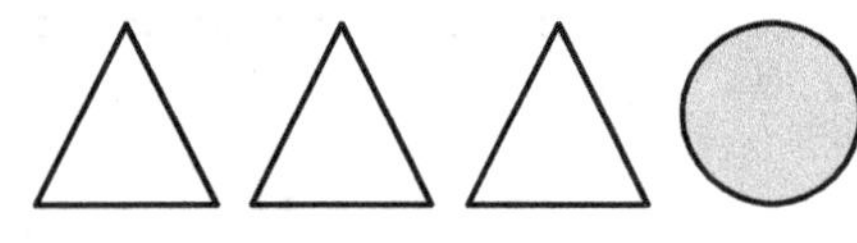

$$3 + 1 = \underline{\phantom{0}}$$

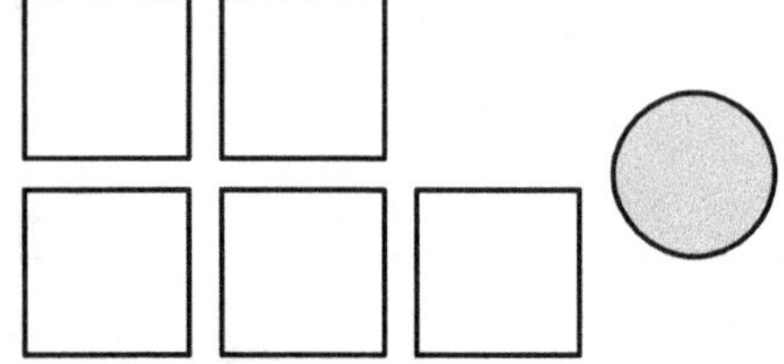

$$5 + 1 = \underline{\phantom{0}}$$

# Subtract a Spider

Trace the numbers and complete the subtraction problems below. Use the pictures to help.

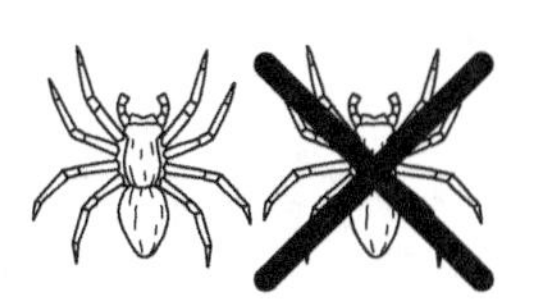

$2 - 1 = 1$

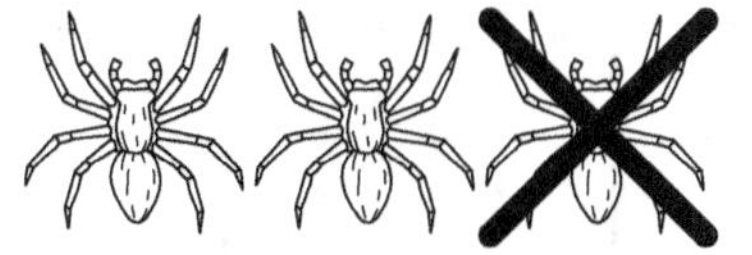

$3 - 1 = 2$

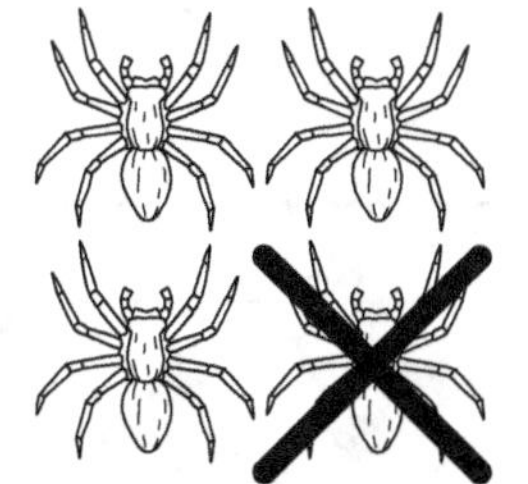

$4 - 1 = \underline{\hspace{1em}}$

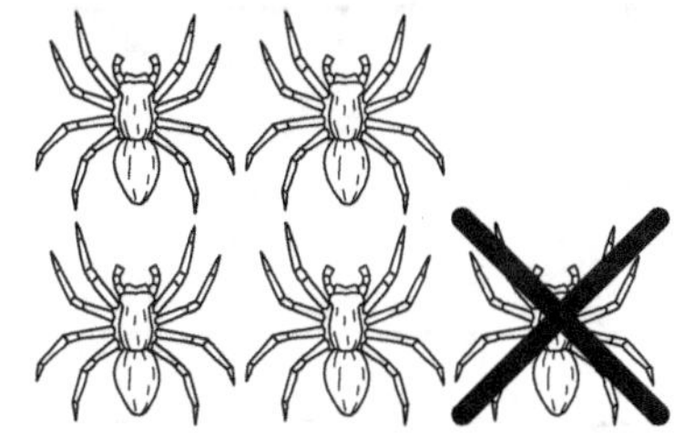

$5 - 1 = \underline{\hspace{1em}}$

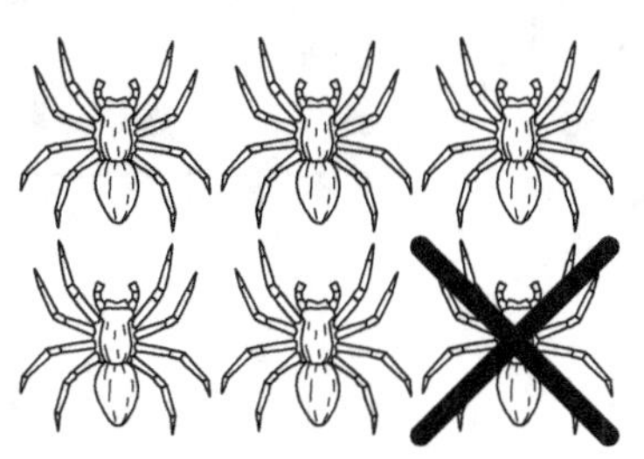

$6 - 1 = \underline{\hspace{1em}}$

## Which One Has More Dots?

Put an X on the domino that has more dots. Trace the numbers below.

3      5      4      2

6      1      0      2

7      5      4      6

6      8      10      9

# Put Them in Order

Use the numbers and dominoes to help with the problems below.

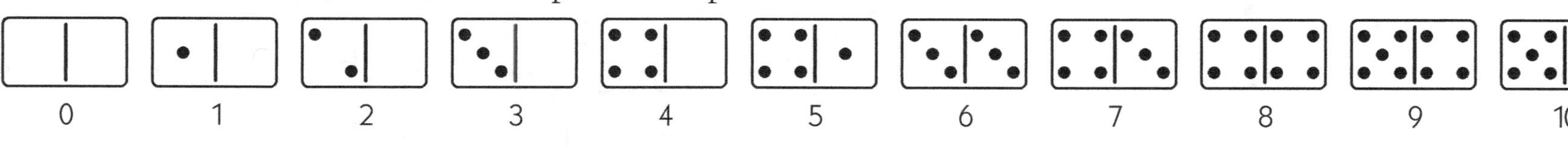

| 0 | 1 | 2 | 3 | 4 | 5 | 6 | 7 | 8 | 9 | 10 |

Trace the numbers. Then write them again in order from least to most.

| 5 | 6 | 4 | | 3 | 1 | 2 |
| 4 | 5 | 6 | | ___ | ___ | ___ |

| 8 | 6 | 7 | | 10 | 8 | 9 |
| ___ | ___ | ___ | | ___ | ___ | ___ |

| 4 | 2 | 3 | | 7 | 9 | 8 |
| ___ | ___ | ___ | | ___ | ___ | ___ |

NAME ______________________ DATE ______________

# Comparing Cube Trains

**1** Trace the numbers.

3 4 5 6 7 8 9

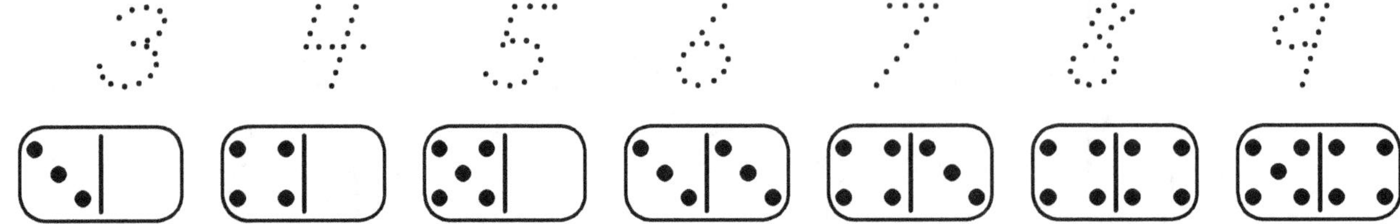

**2** Count the cubes. Write the number to show how many. Draw an X on the train that is longer.

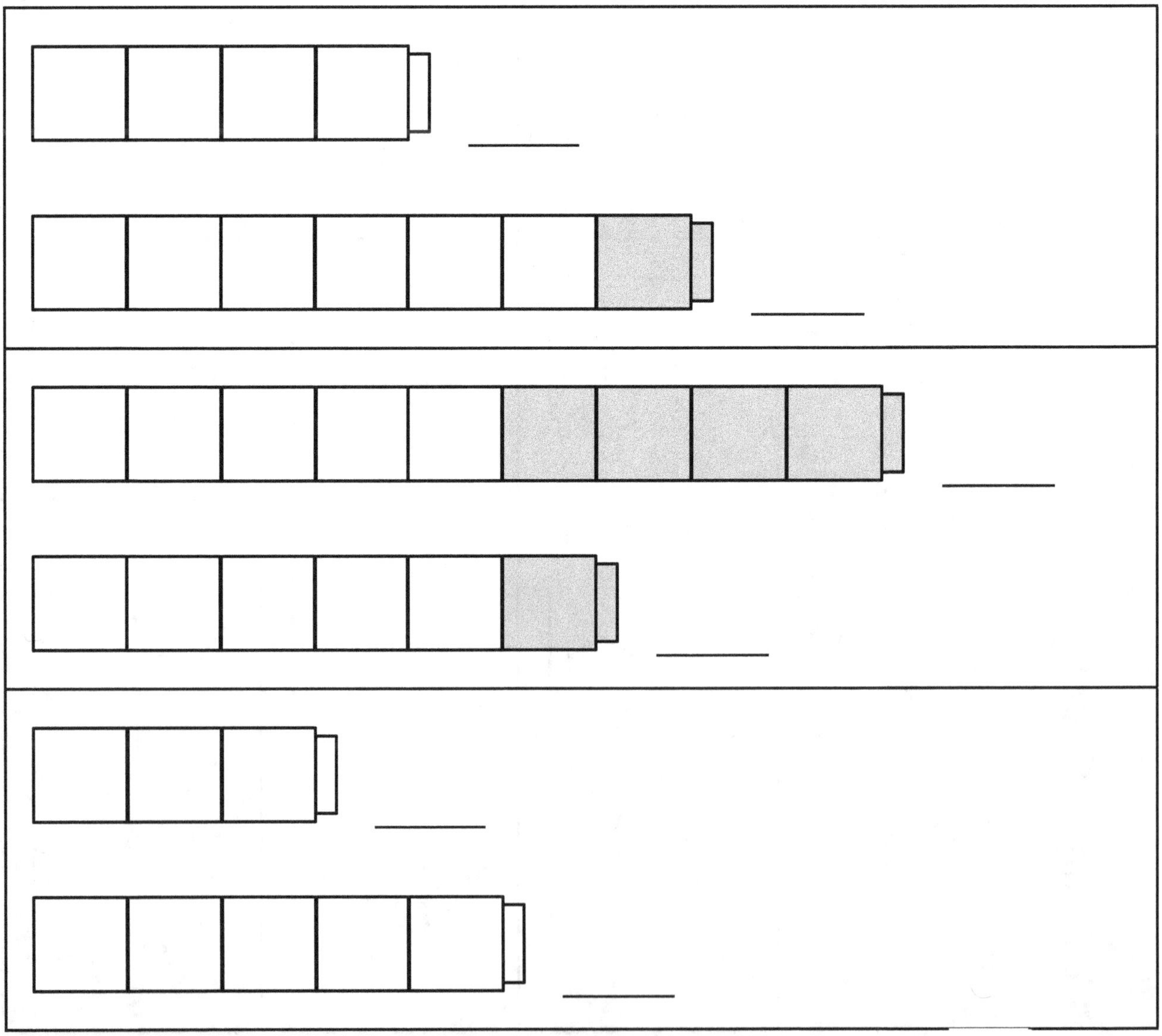

# Which Is Longer? Which Is Shorter?

**1** Draw a red X on the longer pencil. Color the shorter pencil green.

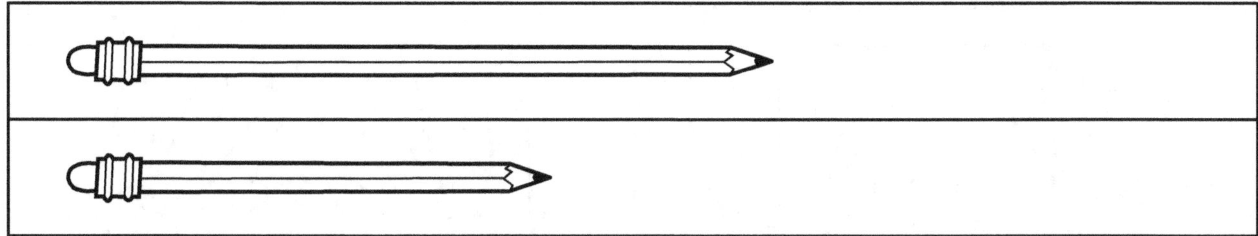

**2** Color the longer vehicle yellow. Draw a circle around the shorter vehicle.

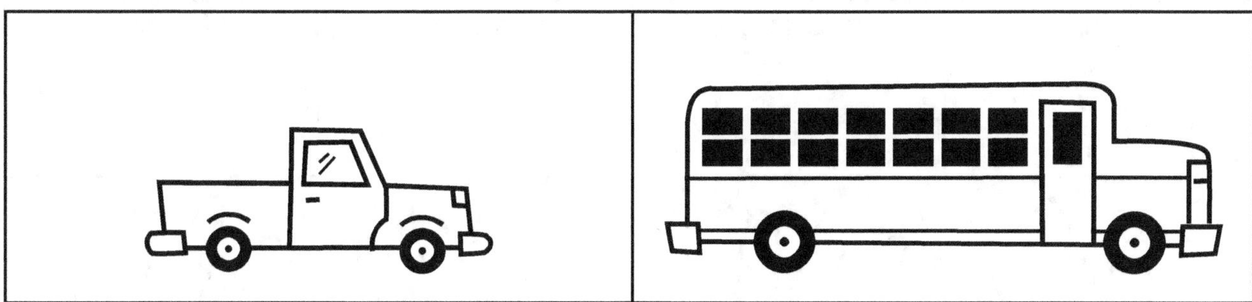

**3** Color the longest ribbon blue. Color the shortest ribbon red.

NAME _______________________________________     DATE _______________

# Comparing Pennies: 0 1 2 3 4 5

**1** How many pennies are there in each hand? Write the number to show. Draw a
blue X on the hand with fewer pennies.

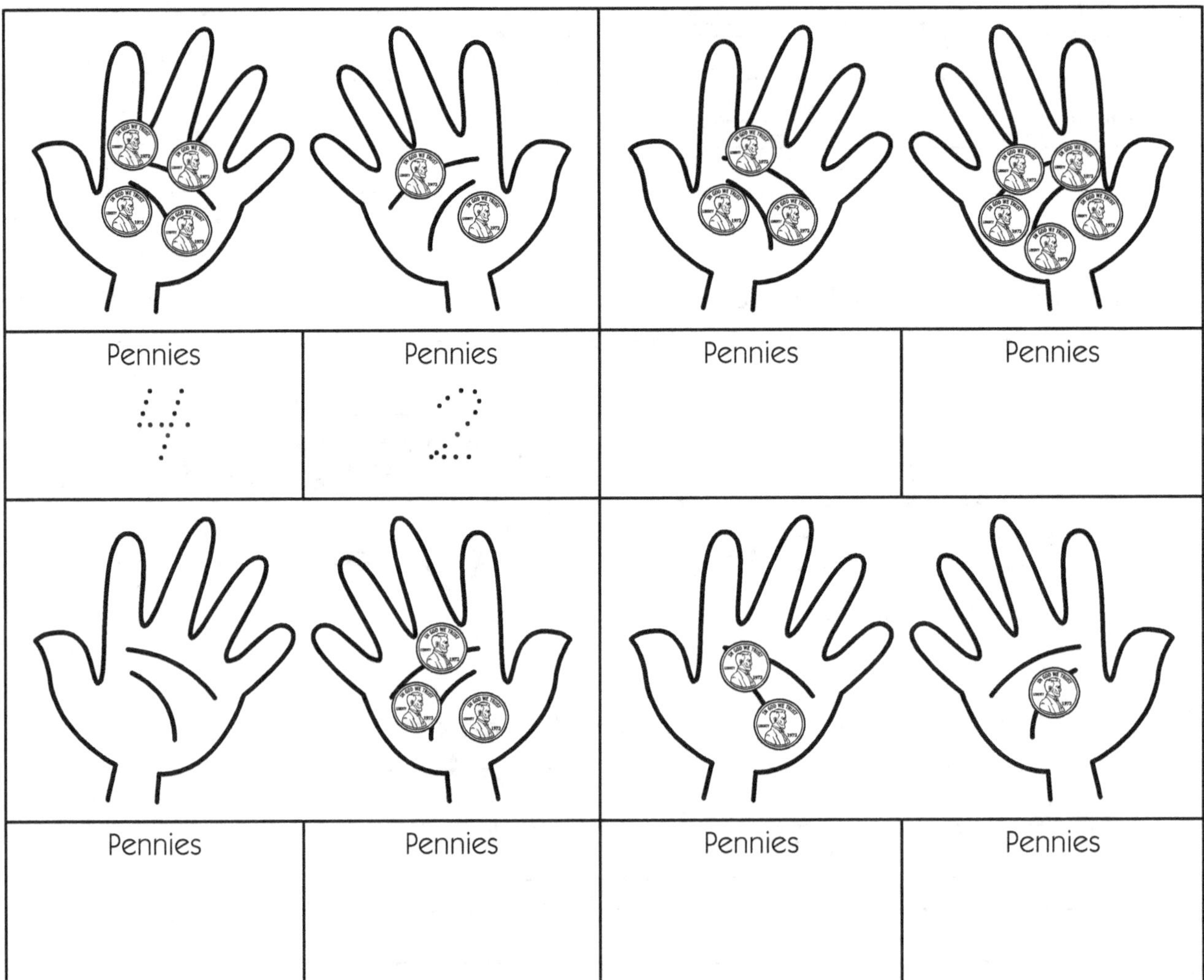


**2** Color the longest ribbon green. Color the shortest ribbon brown.

NAME _________________________________________  DATE _________________________

# Count & Compare Pennies

Count the pennies in each frame. Write how many there are. Then draw lines to the words to show which frame has more and which frame has less.

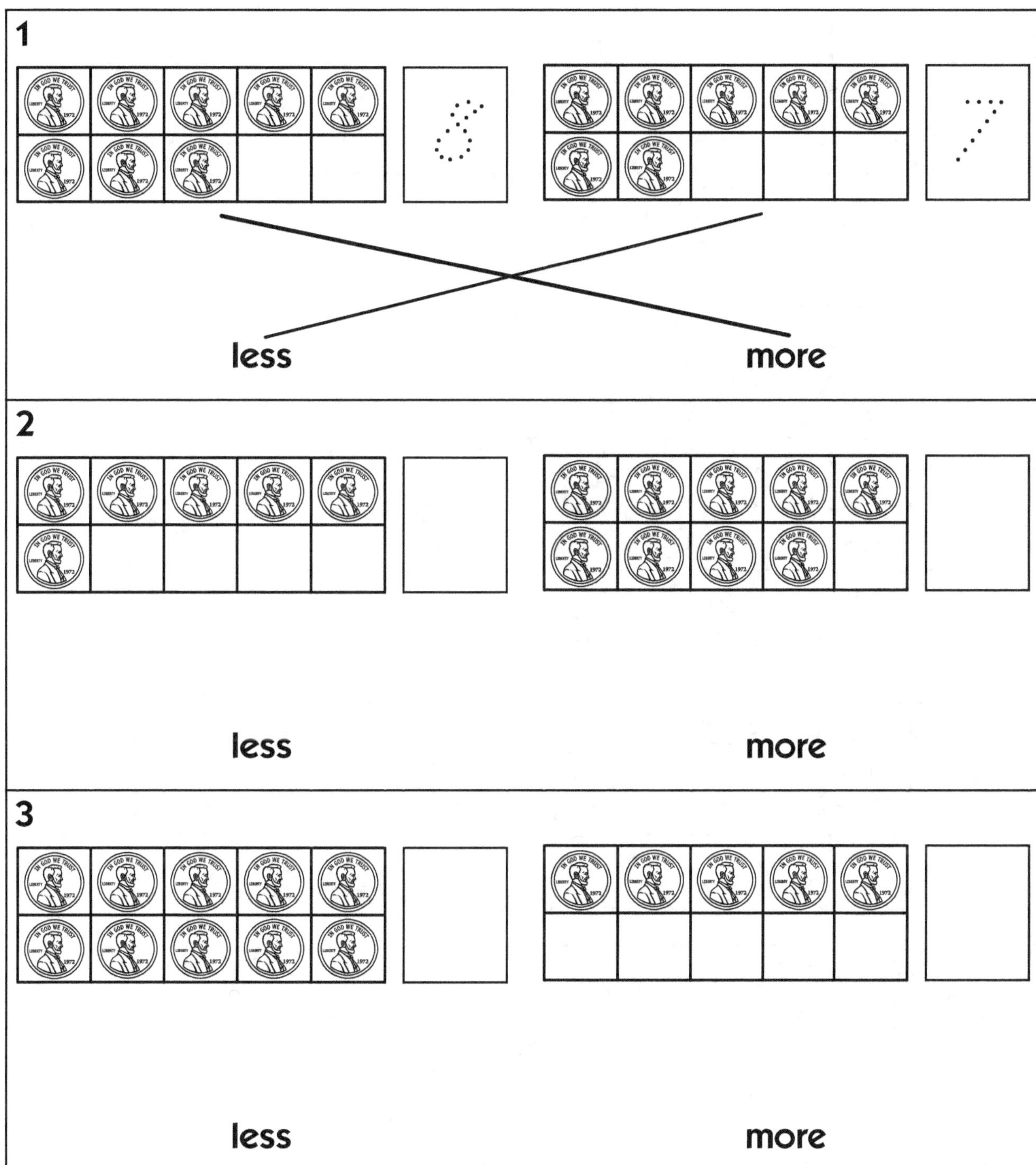

1

less          more

2

less          more

3

less          more

**NAME** _________________________________________________ **DATE** _____________________________

# A Growing Pattern of Ladybugs & Spots

**1** Record the number of ladybugs and spots you see in each row.

| How many ladybugs? | | How many spots? |
|---|---|---|
| one | | |
| two | | |
| three | | |
| four | | |
| five | | |
| six | | |

**2** Circle all of the counting by twos numbers:

| 1 | 2 | 3 | 4 | 5 | 6 | 7 | 8 | 9 | 10 |
|---|---|---|---|---|---|---|---|---|---|
| 11 | 12 | 13 | 14 | 15 | 16 | 17 | 18 | 19 | 20 |
| 21 | 22 | 23 | 24 | 25 | 26 | 27 | 28 | 29 | 30 |

**NAME** ___________________________________________  **DATE** ___________________

# Which Shapes Could It Be?  Sheet 1

Circle all the shapes that fit the clues in each box.

**1**

Clues

_______
straight sides

4 corners

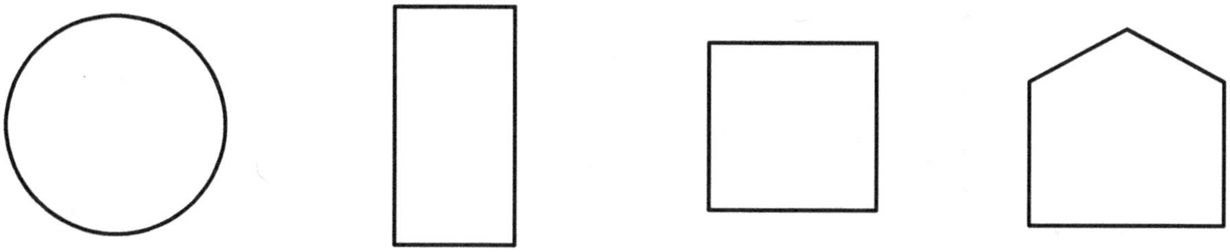

**2**

Clue

curved sides

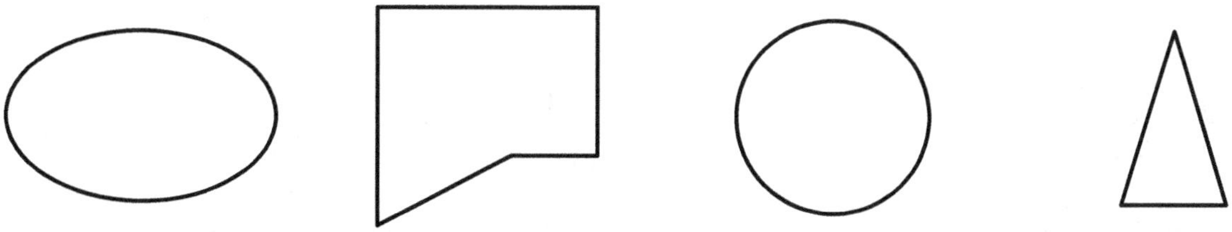

**3**

Clues

_______
straight sides

3 corners

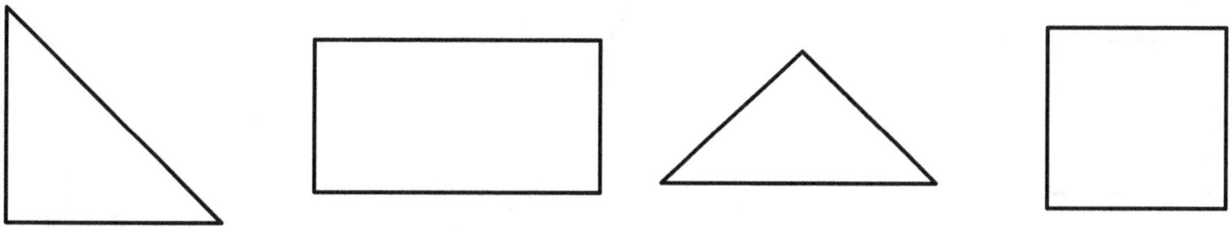

NAME _________________________________    DATE _____________

# Which Shapes Could It Be?  Sheet 2

Color the shape that fits all the clues in each box.

**1**

Clues

______    4 corners    small
straight sides

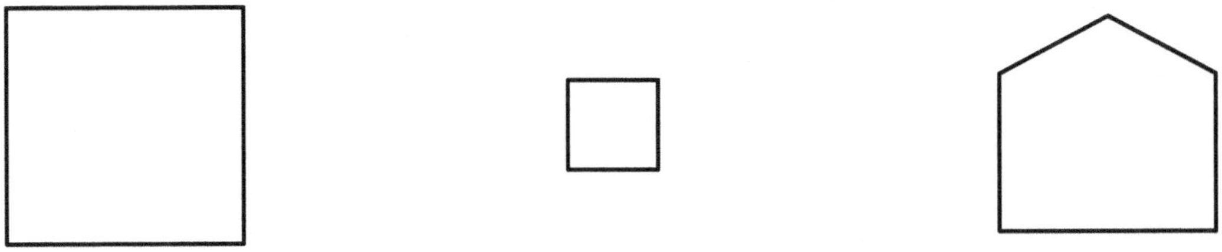

**2**

Clues

curved sides    large

**3**

Clues

______    3 corners    large
straight sides

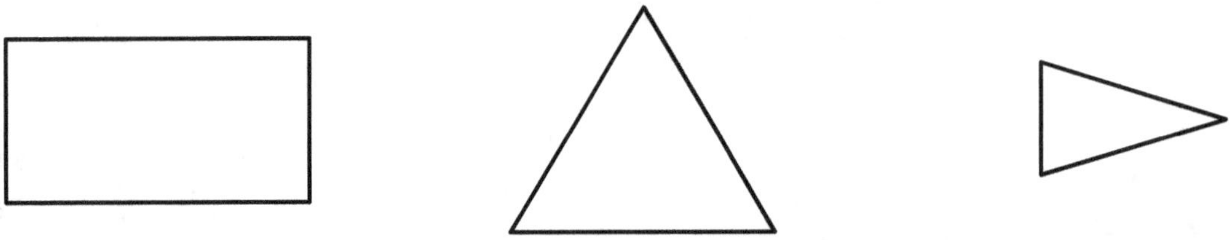

NAME ___________________________________     DATE ___________________

# Line Up Those Numbers

**1** Trace each number. Then write it again in the box below.

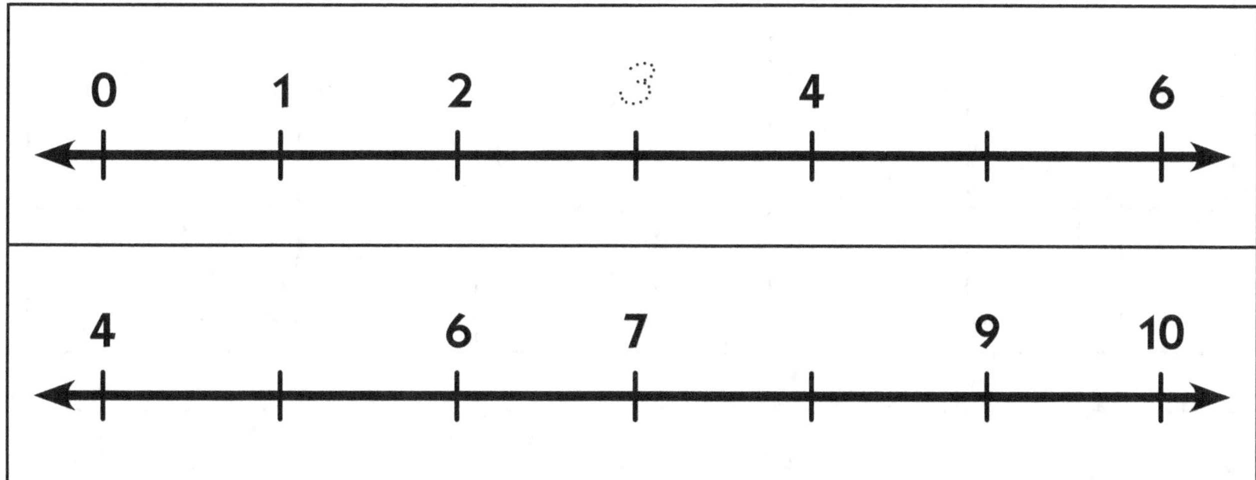

**2** Fill in the missing numbers on the number lines below.

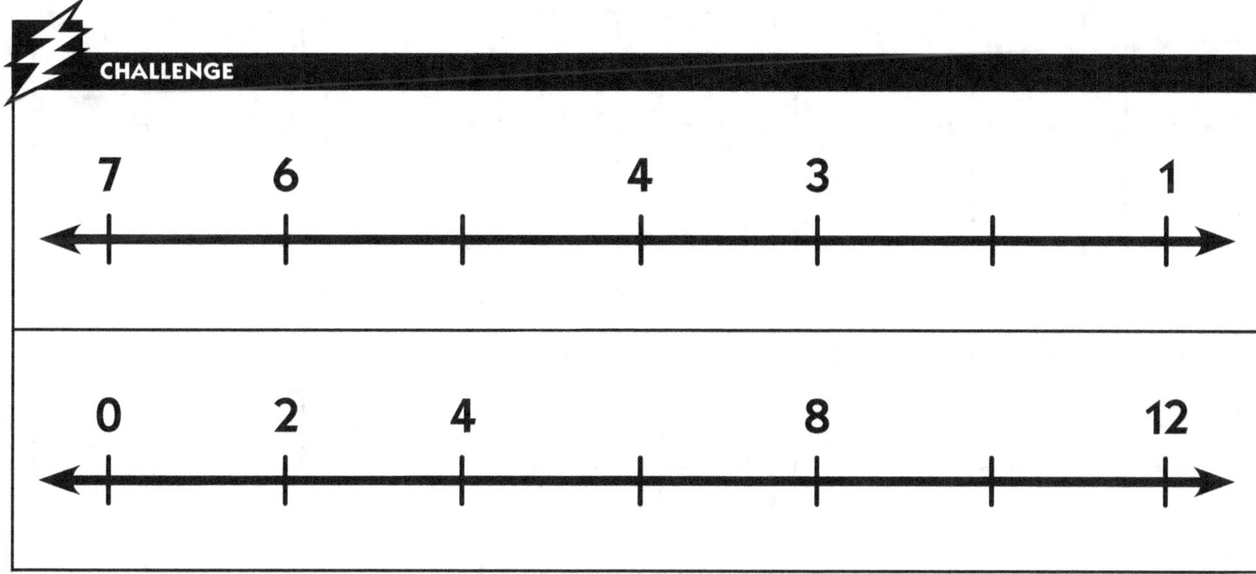

# Coloring Cubes 5–10

Color in the cubes below.

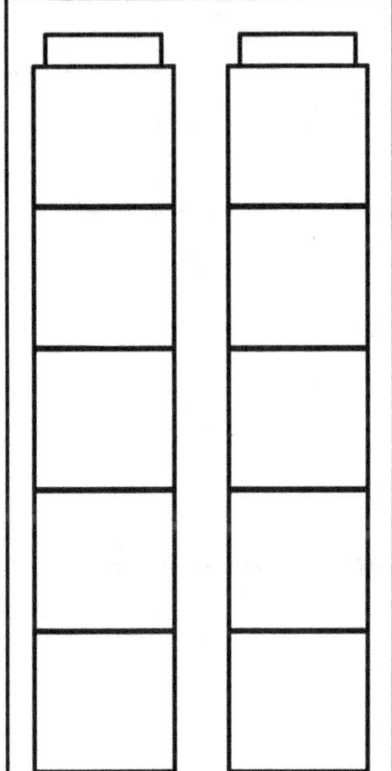


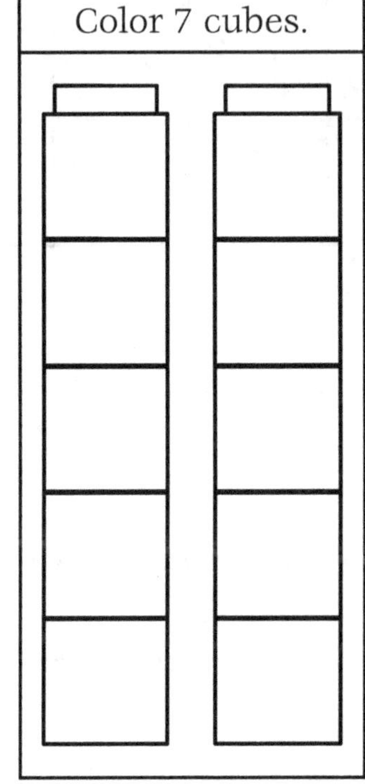


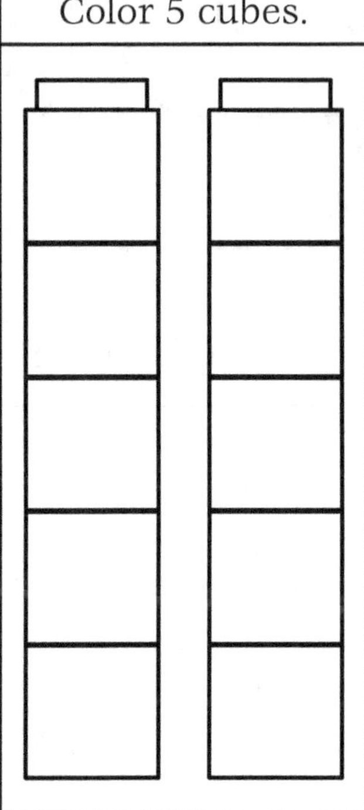


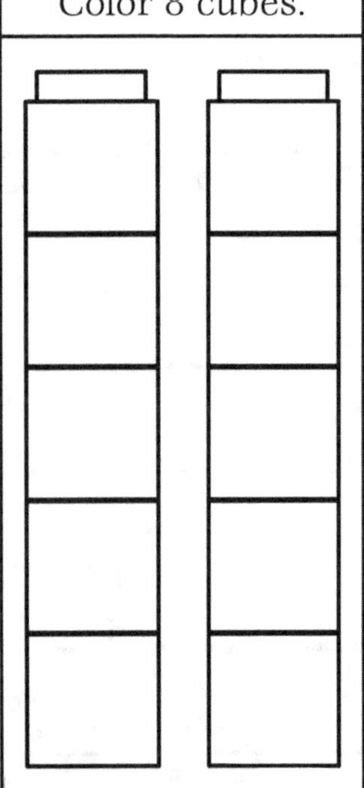


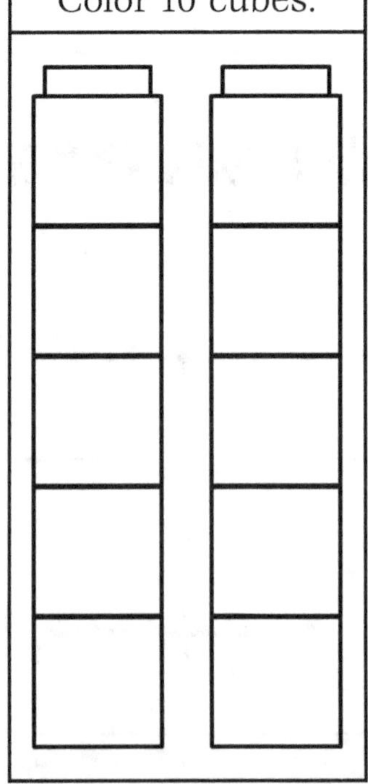


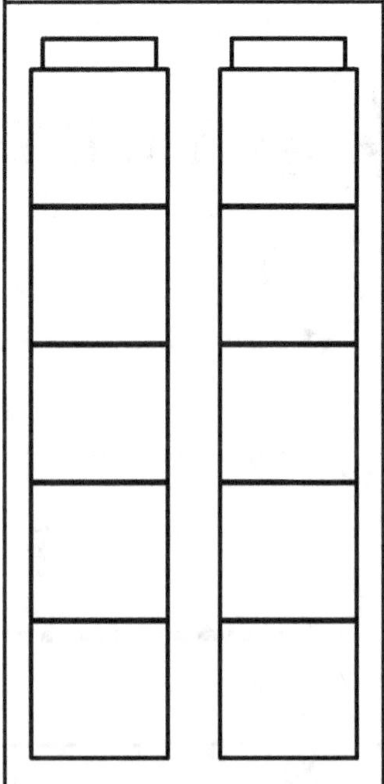

# Dots 11–15

Count the dots in each double ten frame. Trace the numbers.

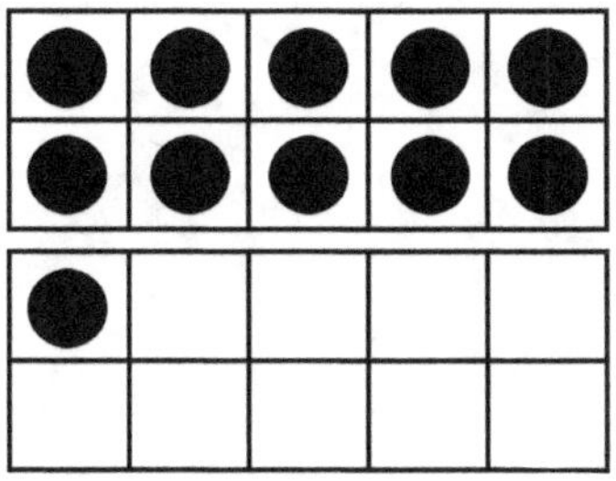

11   11   11

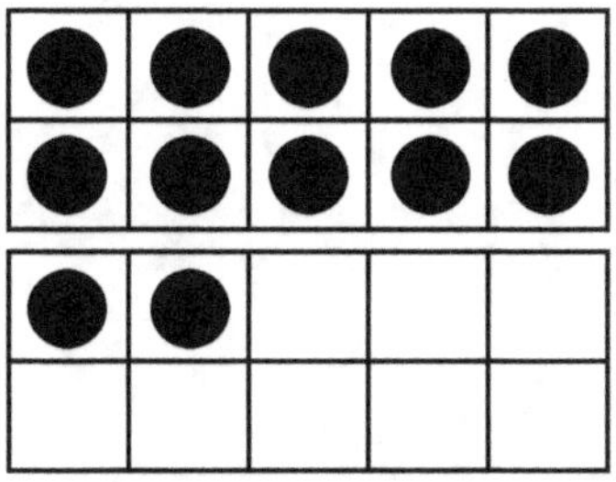

12   12   12

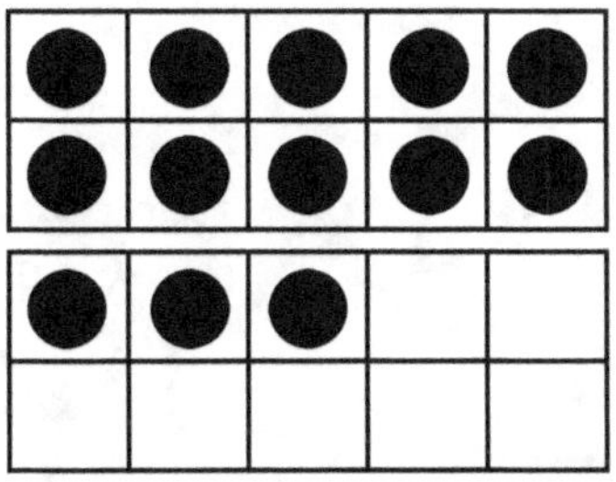

13   13   13

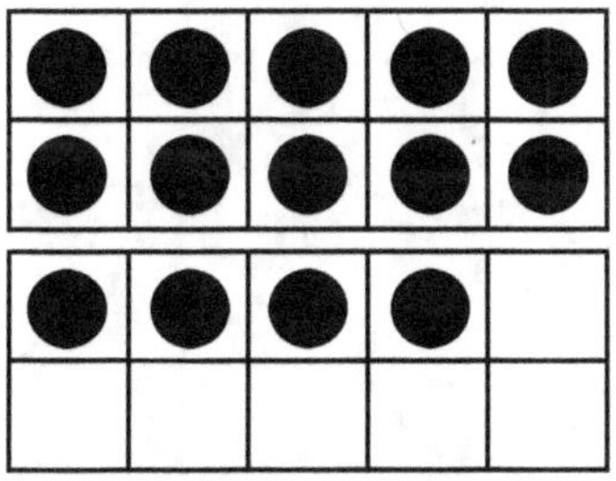

14   14   14

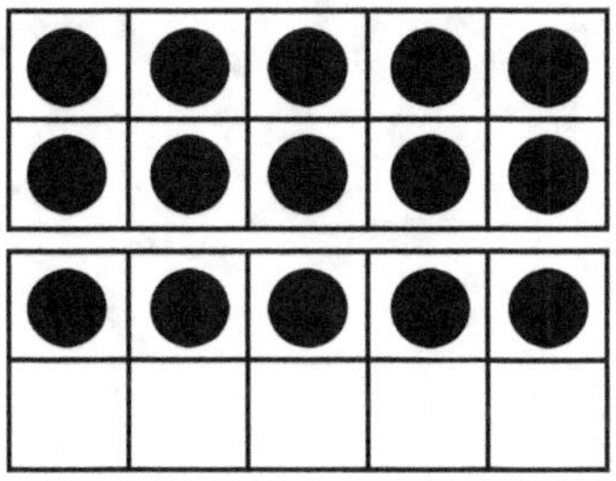

15   15   15

# Dots 16–20

Count the dots in each double ten frame. Trace the numbers.

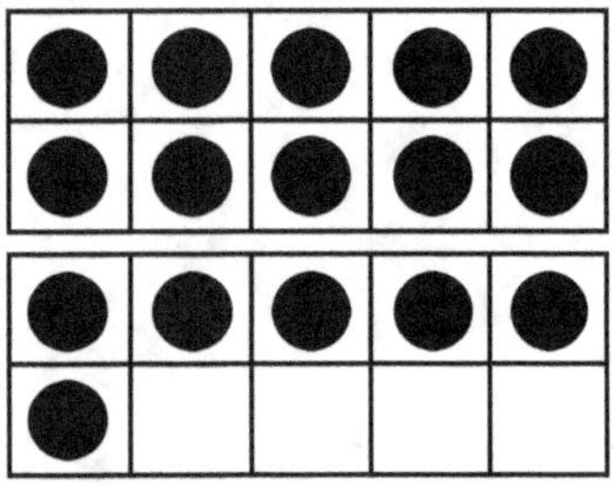

16  16  16

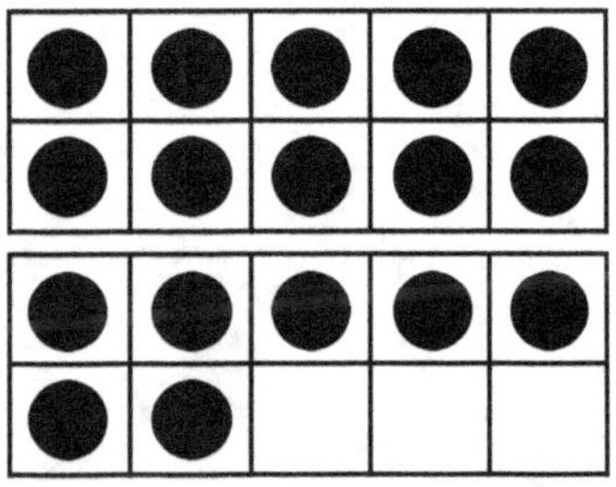

17  17  17

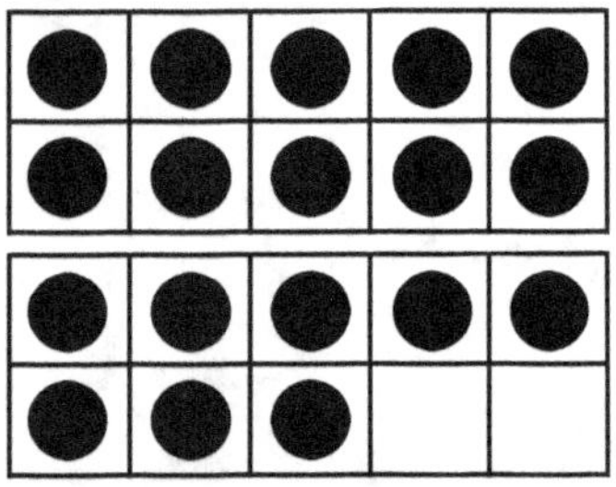

18  18  18

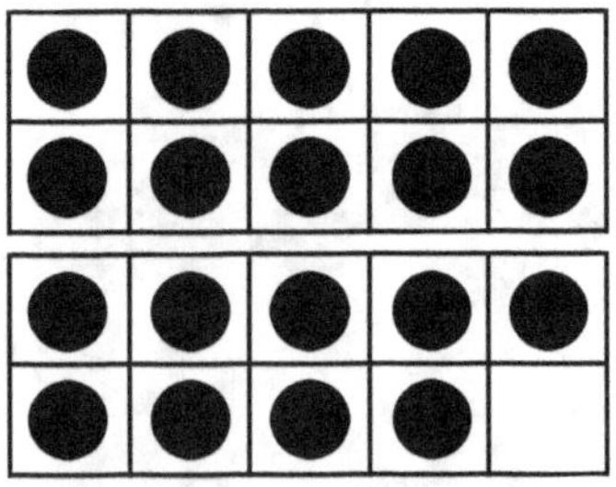

19  19  19

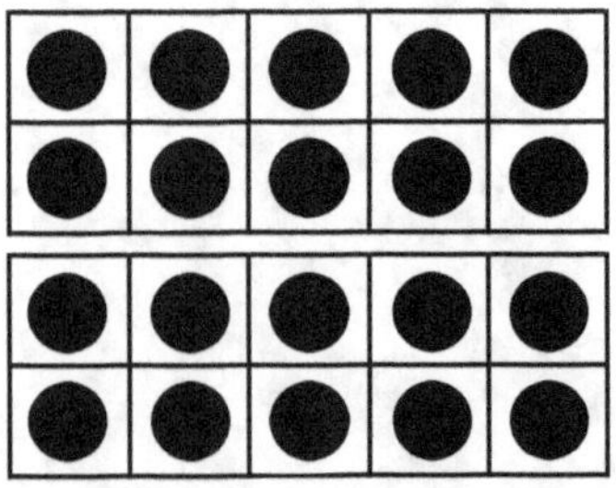

20  20  20

# Count the Dots

**1** Trace each number.

15   16   17   18   19   20

**2** Count the number of dots in each set of double ten frames and record the number.

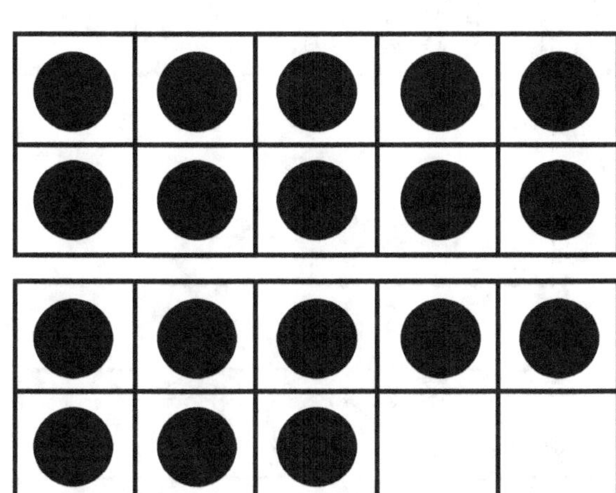

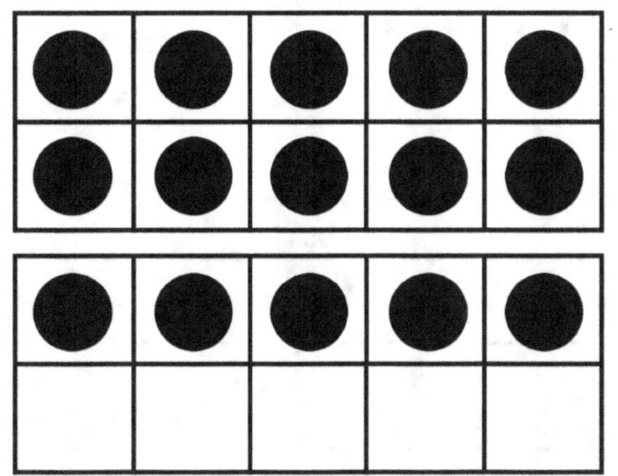

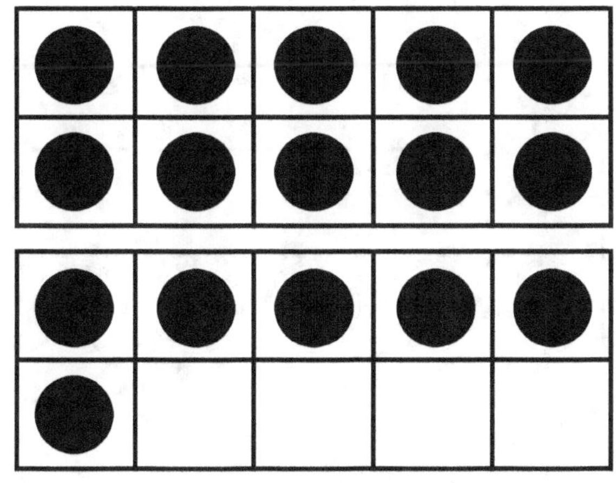

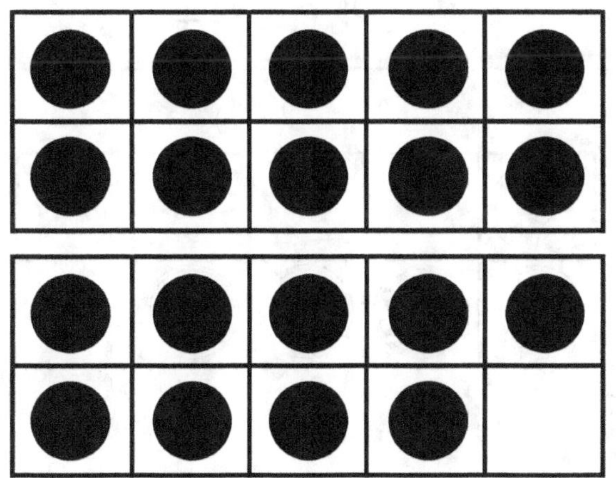

# Add the Pennies

Solve the addition problems. Use the pictures to help.

$$2¢ + 3¢ = \underline{\hspace{2cm}} ¢$$

$$3¢ + 2¢ = \underline{\hspace{2cm}} ¢$$

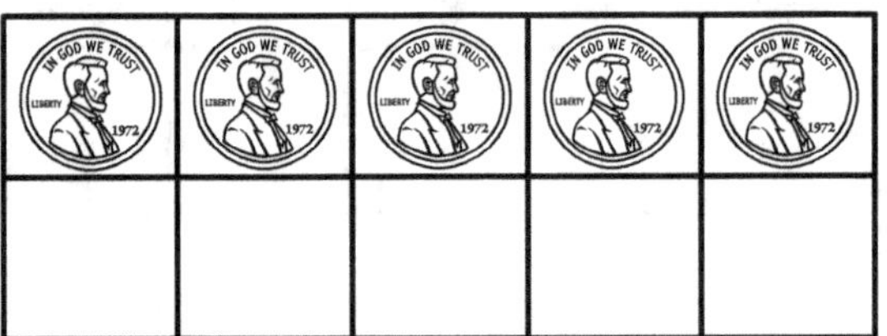

$$5¢ + 0¢ = \underline{\hspace{2cm}} ¢$$

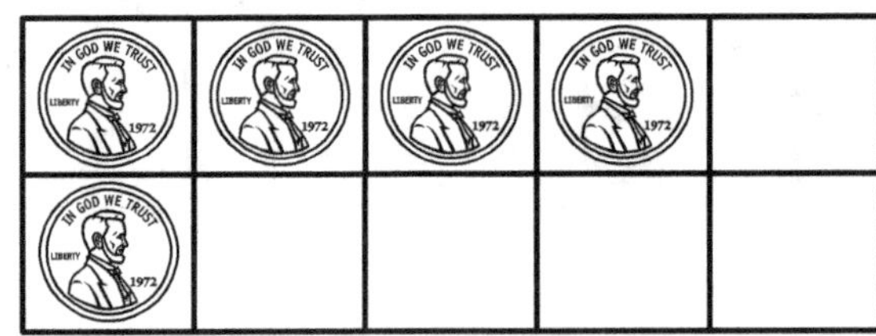

$$4¢ + 1¢ = \underline{\hspace{2cm}} ¢$$

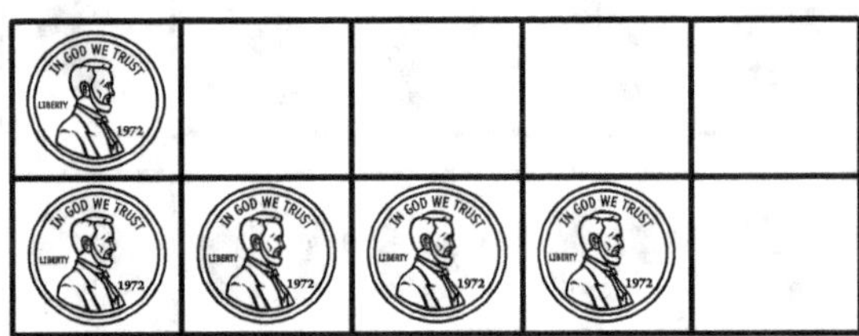

$$1¢ + 4¢ = \underline{\hspace{2cm}} ¢$$

$$0¢ + 5¢ = \underline{\hspace{2cm}} ¢$$

NAME ______________________ DATE ______________

# Make 4

**1** Color the cubes to match each equation.

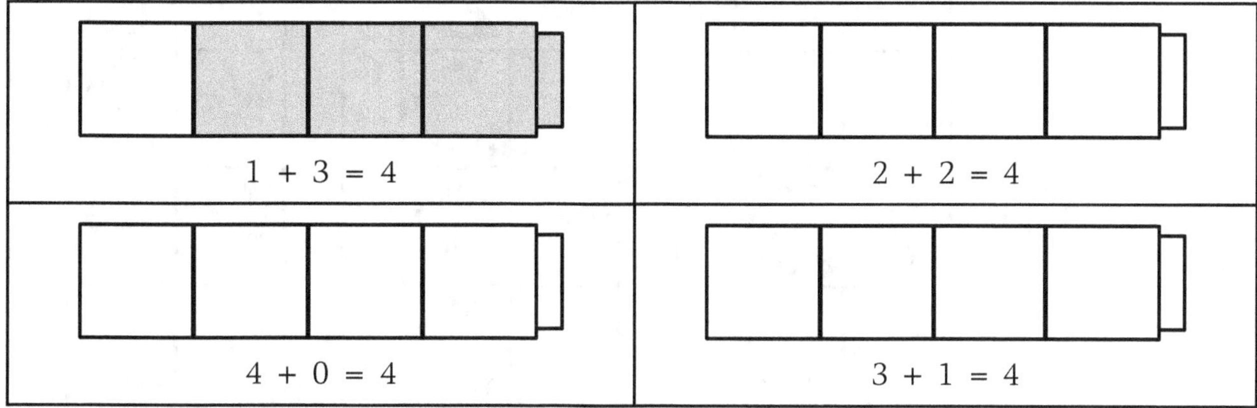

1 + 3 = 4

2 + 2 = 4

4 + 0 = 4

3 + 1 = 4

**2** Trace the numbers and solve the problems. Use the pictures to help.

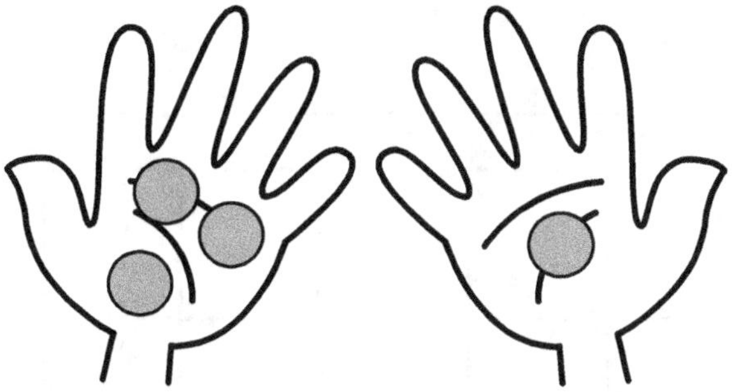

3 + 1 = ____

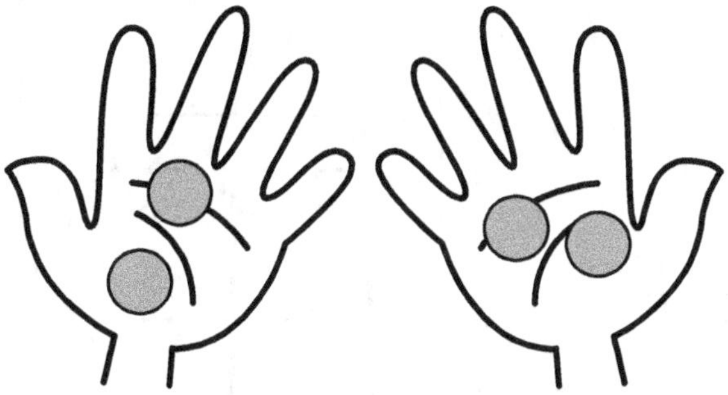

2 + 2 = ____

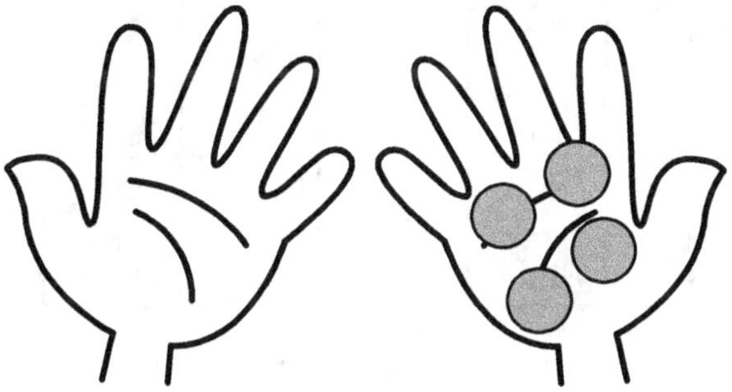

0 + 4 = ____

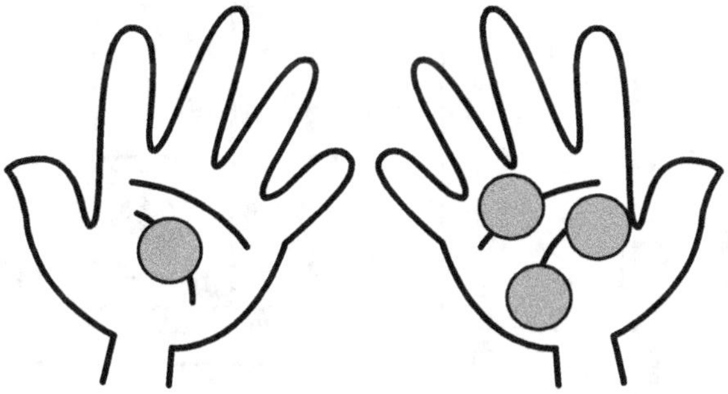

____ + ____ = 4

NAME ____________________ DATE ____________

# How Many Insects? Add Them Up

Solve the addition problems. Use the pictures to help.

| | | | |
|---|---|---|---|
| $\begin{array}{r} 1 \\ +\ 1 \\ \hline 2 \end{array}$ | 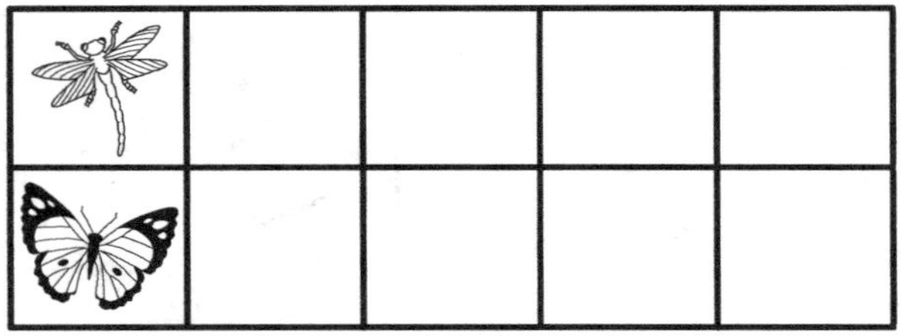 | $\begin{array}{r} 2 \\ +\ 2 \\ \hline \end{array}$ | 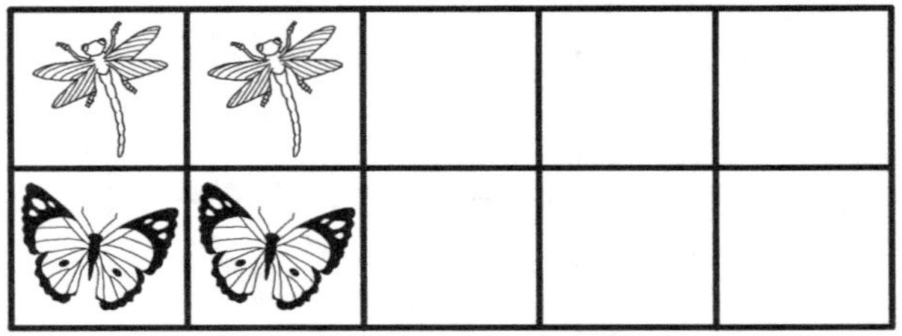 |
| $\begin{array}{r} 3 \\ +\ 3 \\ \hline \end{array}$ | 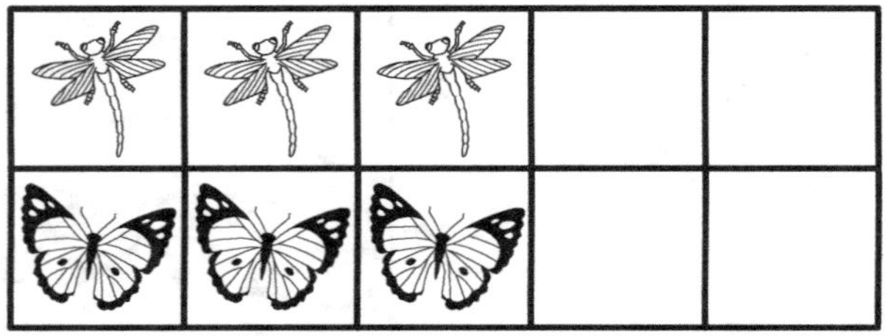 | $\begin{array}{r} 4 \\ +\ 4 \\ \hline \end{array}$ | 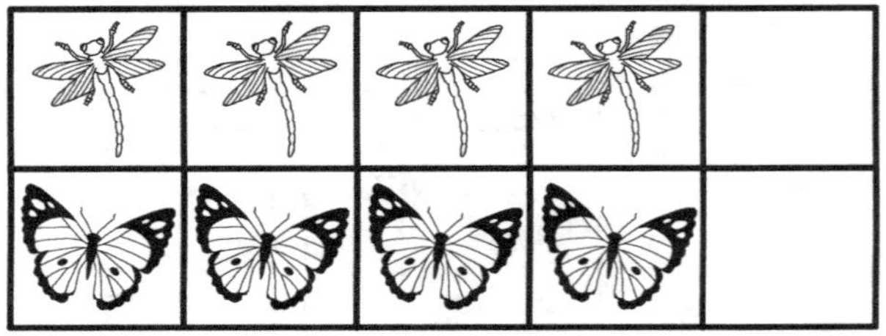 |
| $\begin{array}{r} 4 \\ +\ 4 \\ \hline \end{array}$ | 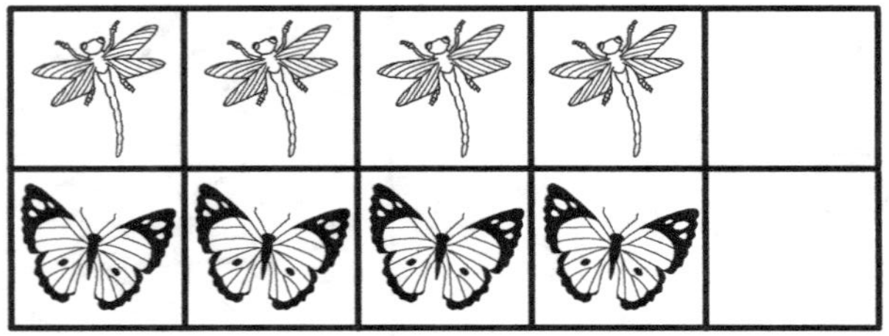 | $\begin{array}{r} 5 \\ +\ 5 \\ \hline \end{array}$ | 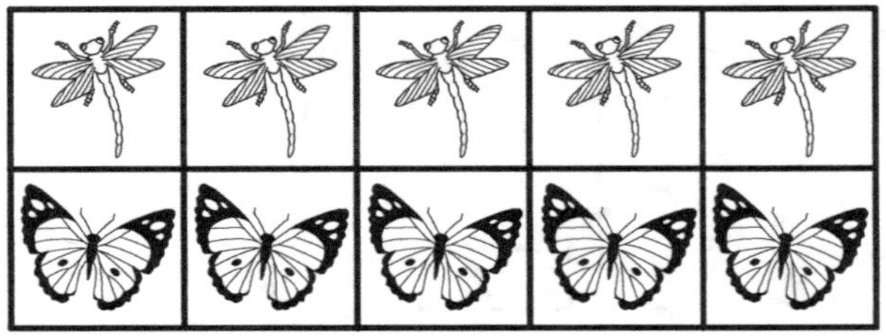 |

## A Story Problem

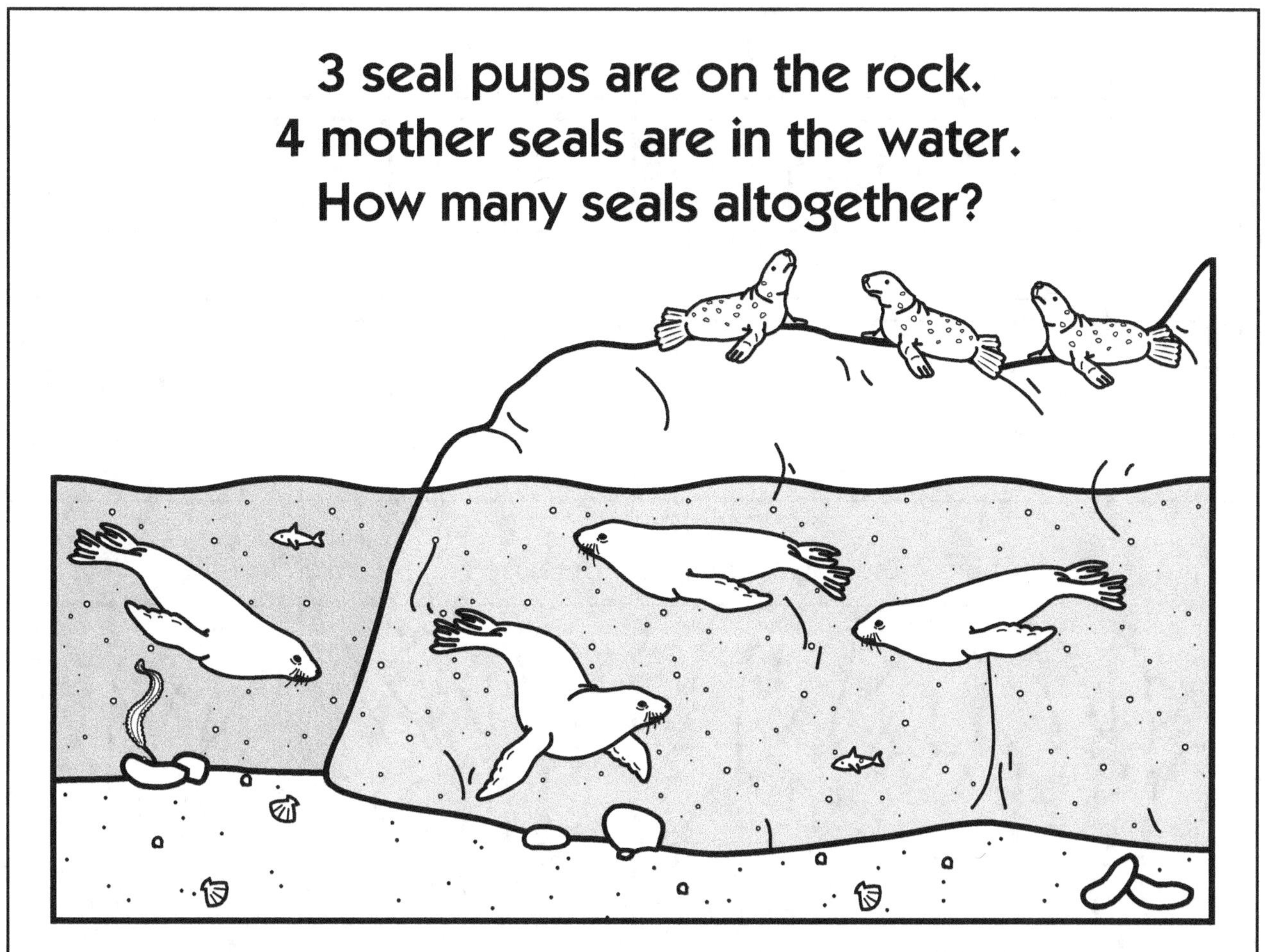



Use pictures and numbers to show how you solve the problem.

NAME ______________________ DATE ______________

# Make 5

**1** Color the cubes to match each equation.

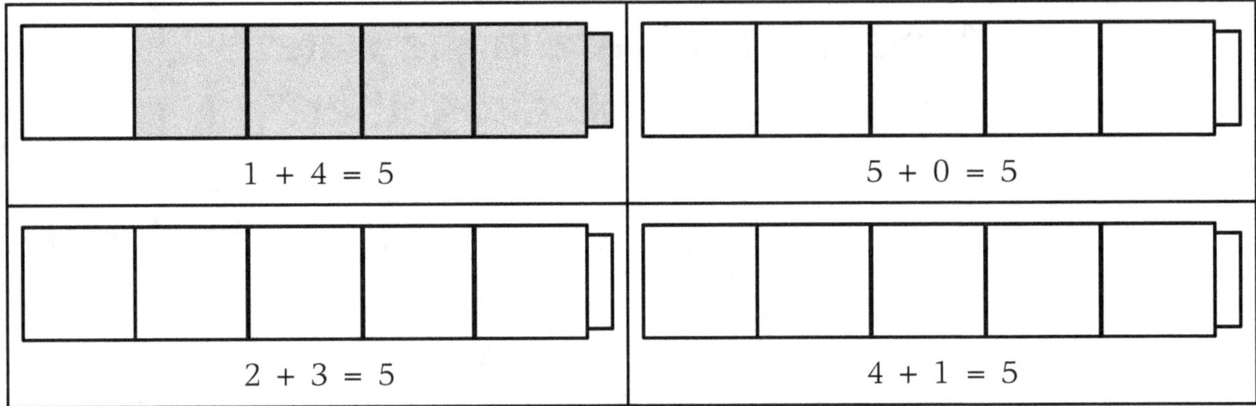

| | |
|---|---|
|  1 + 4 = 5 |  5 + 0 = 5 |
|  2 + 3 = 5 |  4 + 1 = 5 |

**2** Trace the numbers and solve the problems. Use the pictures to help.

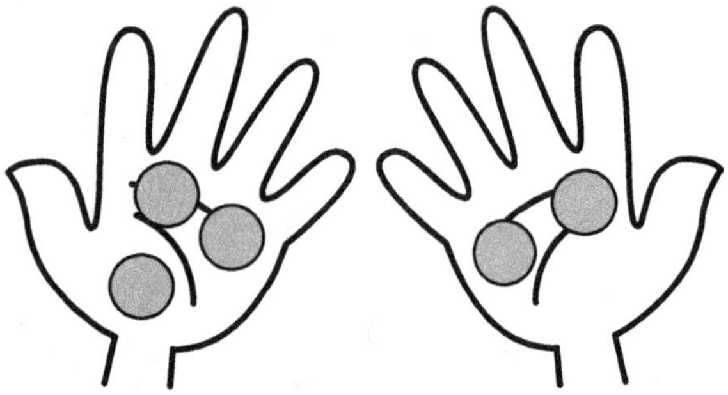

| | |
|---|---|
|  3 + 2 = ____ |  4 + 1 = ____ |
|  0 + 5 = ____ |  ____ + ____ = 5 |

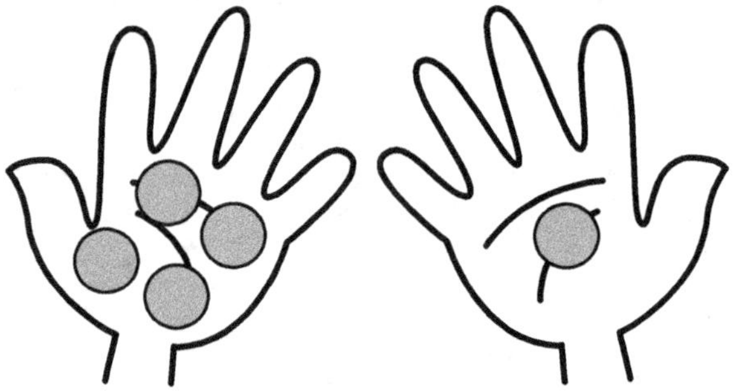

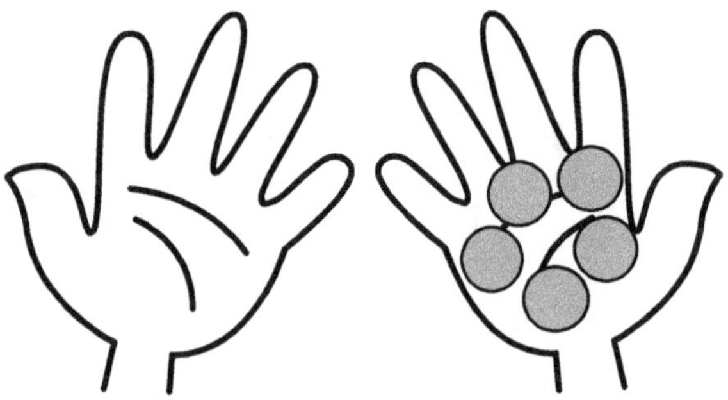

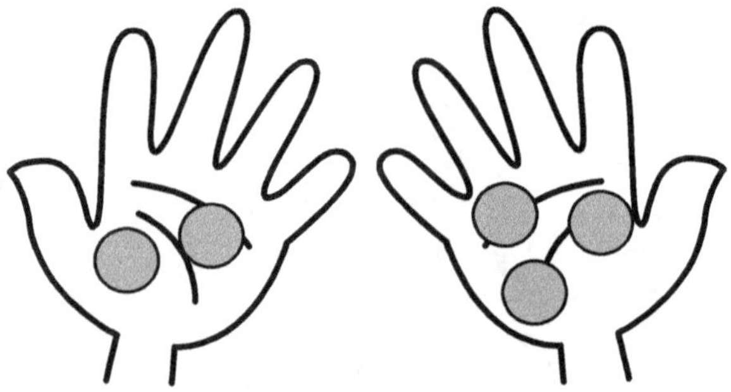

# Counting Dimes

Use the following information to help solve the problems below.

**1** Trace the numbers.

**2** How many cents? Write the amount.

| | |
|---|---|
| (1 dime) | _10_ ¢ |
| (2 dimes) | ____ ¢ |
| (3 dimes) | ____ ¢ |
| (4 dimes) | ____ ¢ |
| (5 dimes) | ____ ¢ |

NAME ______________________ DATE ______________

# Make 6

**1** Color the cubes to match each equation.

1 + 5 = 6

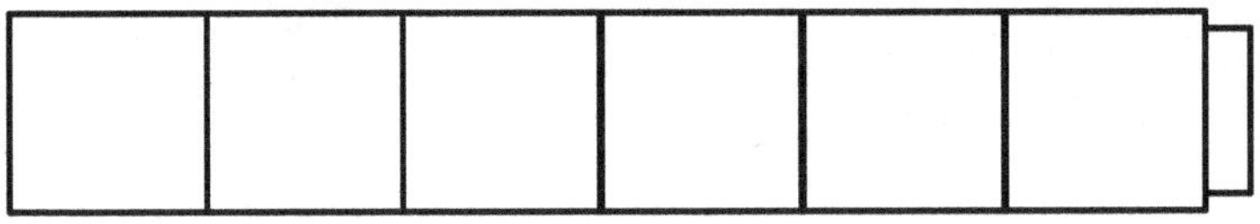

2 + 4 = 6

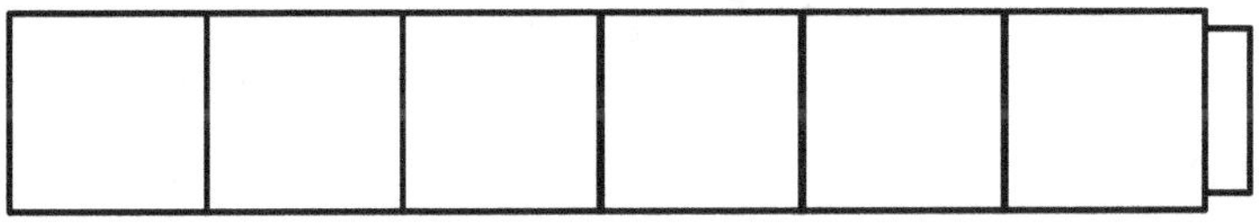

3 + 3 = 6

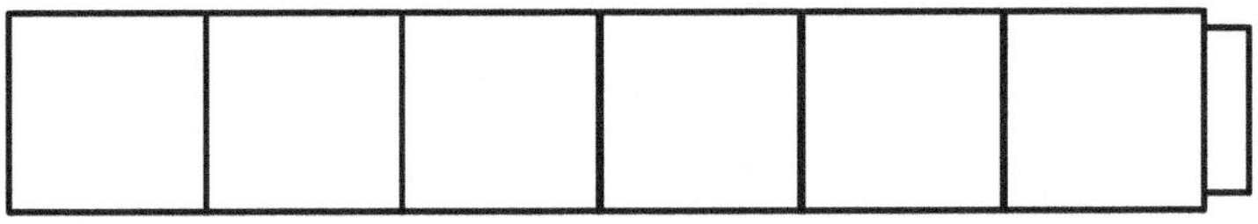

6 + 0 = 6

**2** Trace the numbers and solve the problems. Use the pictures to help.

_____ + _____ = 6

_____ + _____ = 6

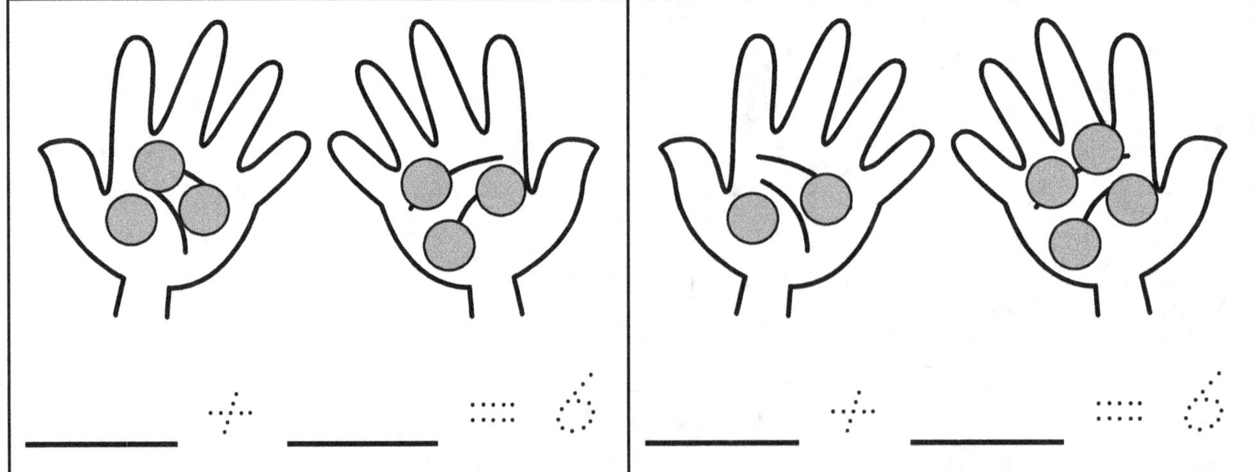

# Hot or Cold Weather?

**1** Circle each picture that shows hot weather. Put a line under each picture that shows cold weather.

**2** Draw a picture to go with the descriptions below.

| Here is something I like to do when it's hot outside. | Here is something I like to do when it's cold outside. |
| --- | --- |
|  |  |

NAME ______________________ DATE __________

# Count the Cubes

**1** Trace each number.

10 11 12 13 14 15

**2** Count the cubes in each set and record the number.

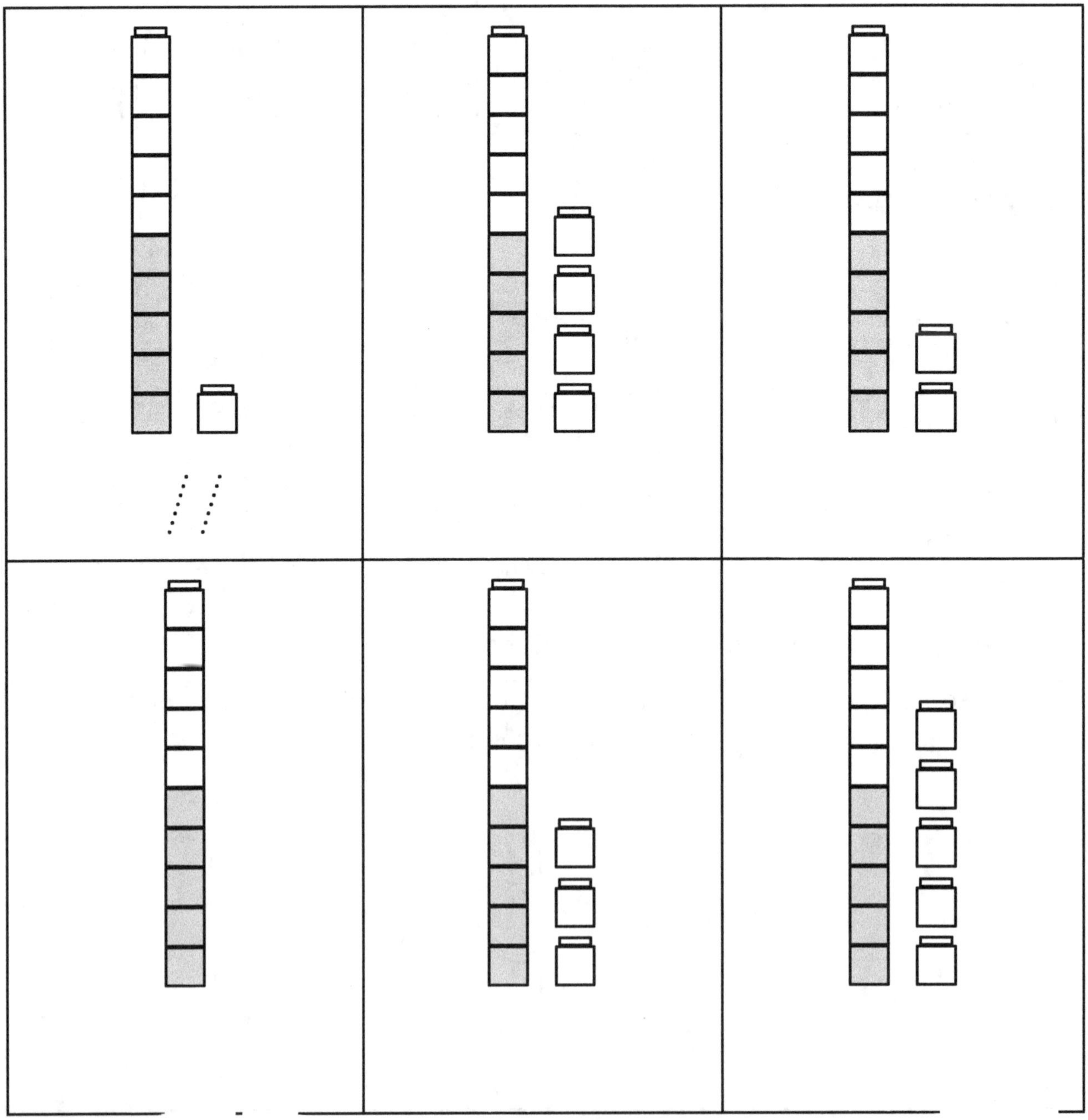

# Tens & Ones  How Many?

How many cubes in each set? Write the number to show.

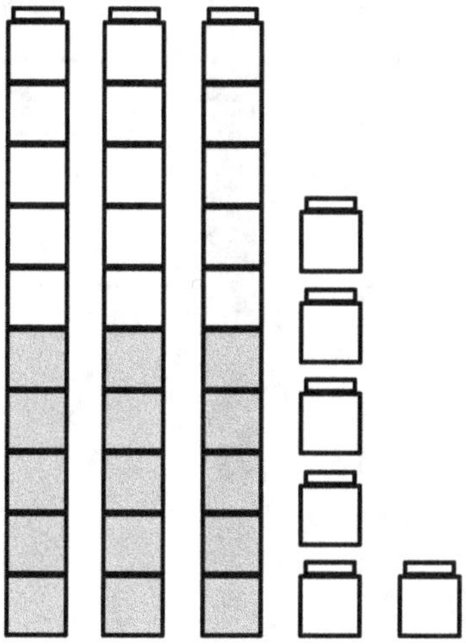

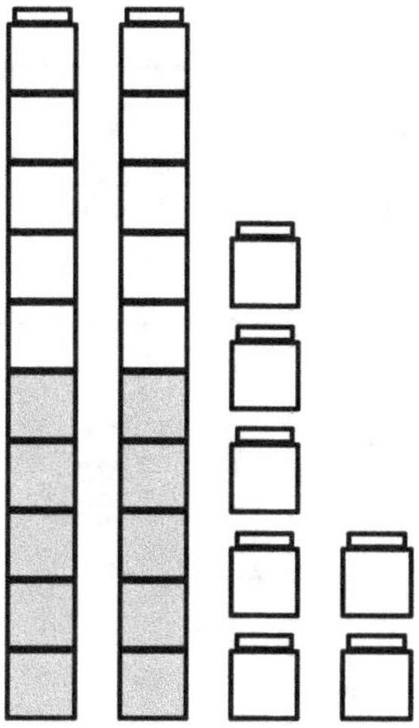

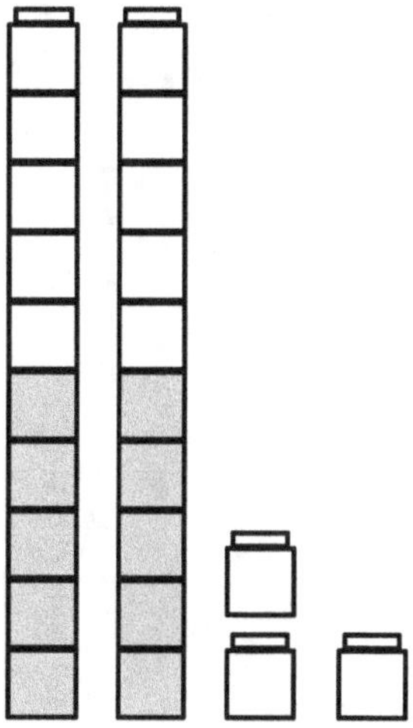

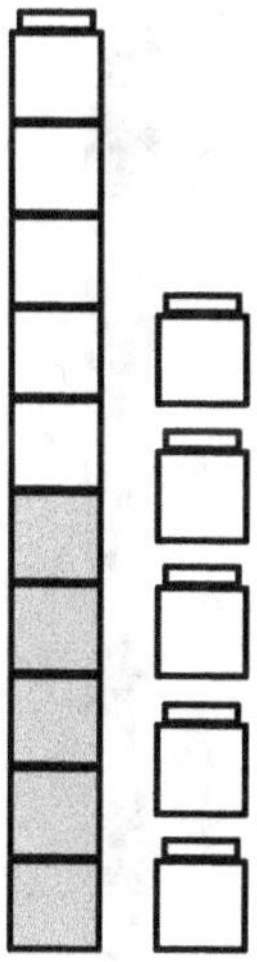

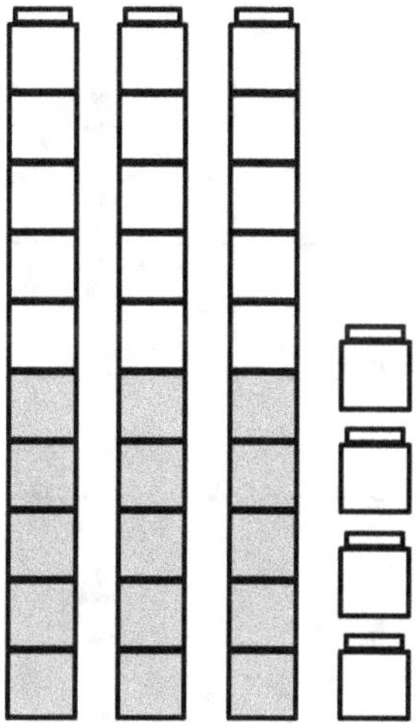

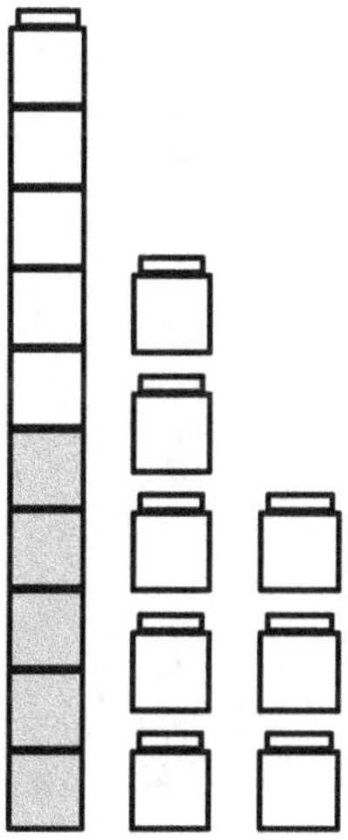

# What's Missing?  Sheet 1

**1** Trace each number.

*1 2 3 4 5 6 7 8 9 10*

**2** Fill in the mising numbers.

| 1 | 2 | 3 |  | 5 | 6 | 7 |  | 9 | 10 |
|---|---|---|---|---|---|---|---|---|----|
| 11 | 12 |  | 14 | 15 |  | 17 | 18 |  | 20 |
| 21 |  | 23 |  | 25 | 26 |  |  | 29 | 30 |

| 31 |  |  |  | 35 |  | 37 |  |  | 40 |
|----|---|---|---|----|---|----|---|---|----|

## What's Missing?  Sheet 2

**1** Fill in the missing numbers on this calendar.

| Sunday | Monday | Tuesday | Wednesday | Thursday | Friday | Saturday |
|--------|--------|---------|-----------|----------|--------|----------|
|  |  |  |  | 1 | 2 | 3 |
| 4 |  | 6 | 7 | 8 |  | 10 |
| 11 | 12 |  | 14 |  | 16 | 17 |
| 18 |  | 20 | 21 |  | 23 |  |
| 25 |  | 27 |  | 29 |  | 31 |

**2** How many days are there in a week?

# Calendar Markers

**1** The shapes on the calendar form a repeating pattern but some are missing. Fill them in.

| Sunday | Monday | Tuesday | Wednesday | Thursday | Friday | Saturday |
|---|---|---|---|---|---|---|
| | ◯ <br> **1** | ▭ <br> **2** | ▭ <br> **3** | ◯ <br> **4** | ▭ <br> **5** | ▭ <br> **6** |
| ◯ <br> **7** | ▭ <br> **8** | ▭ <br> **9** | ◯ <br> **10** | ▭ <br> **11** | ▭ <br> **12** | **13** |
| ▭ <br> **14** | **15** | **16** | ▭ <br> **17** | ▭ <br> **18** | **19** | ▭ <br> **20** |
| ▭ <br> **21** | ◯ <br> **22** | ▭ <br> **23** | **24** | ◯ <br> **25** | **26** | ▭ <br> **27** |
| ◯ <br> **28** | **29** | ▭ <br> **30** | **31** | | | |

**2** How many days are there in a week?

# Cats & Dogs Addition

Fill in the numbers and then solve the addition problem. Use the pictures to help.

**1**

________ Cats    +    ________ Dogs    =    ________

**2**

________ Cats    +    ________ Dog    =    ________

**3**

________ Cats    +    ________ Dogs    =    ________

# Frog & Toad Probability

**1** Frog got 6 spins. Toad got 4 spins. Color the graph to show.

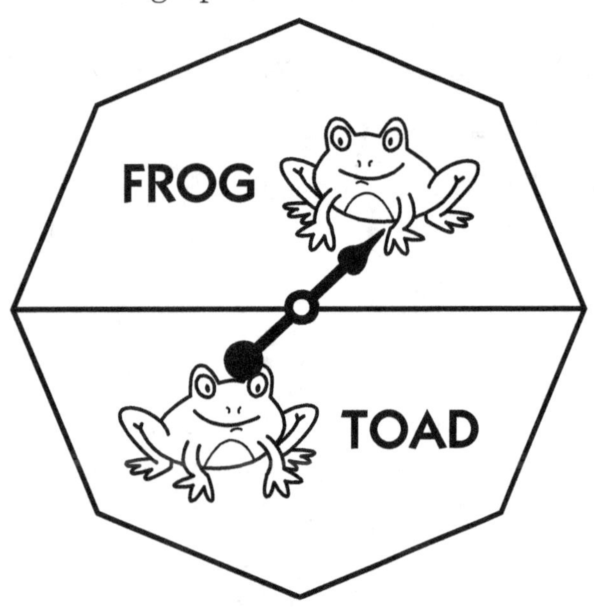


**2** How many more spins did Frog get than Toad?

**3** How many spins did Frog and Toad get in all?

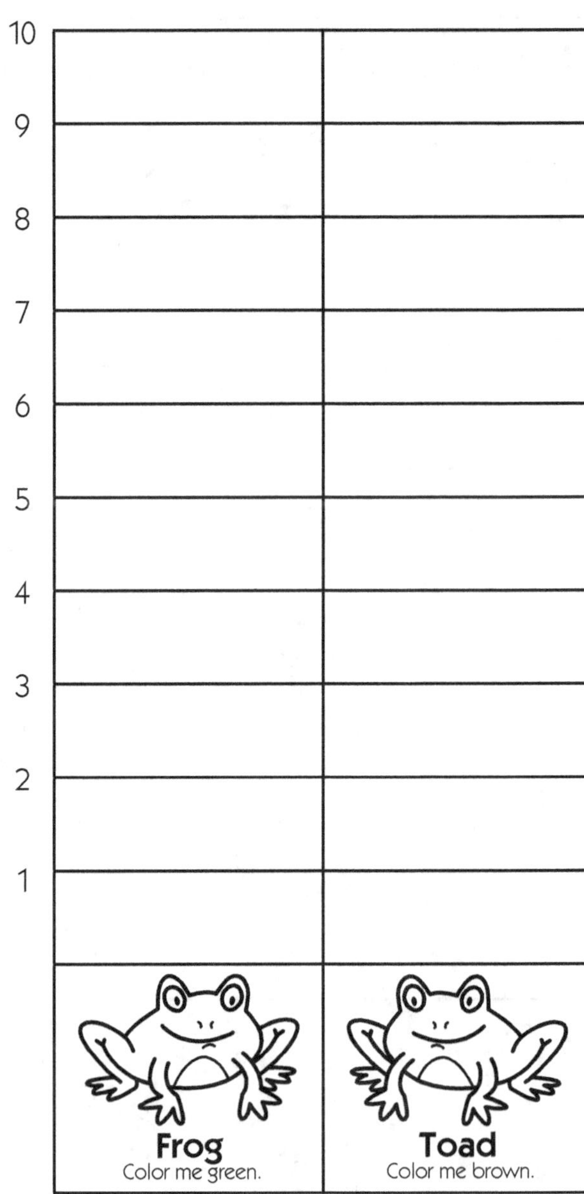

NAME ______________________ DATE ______________

# What Time Is It?

Draw lines to connect the clocks and time cards.

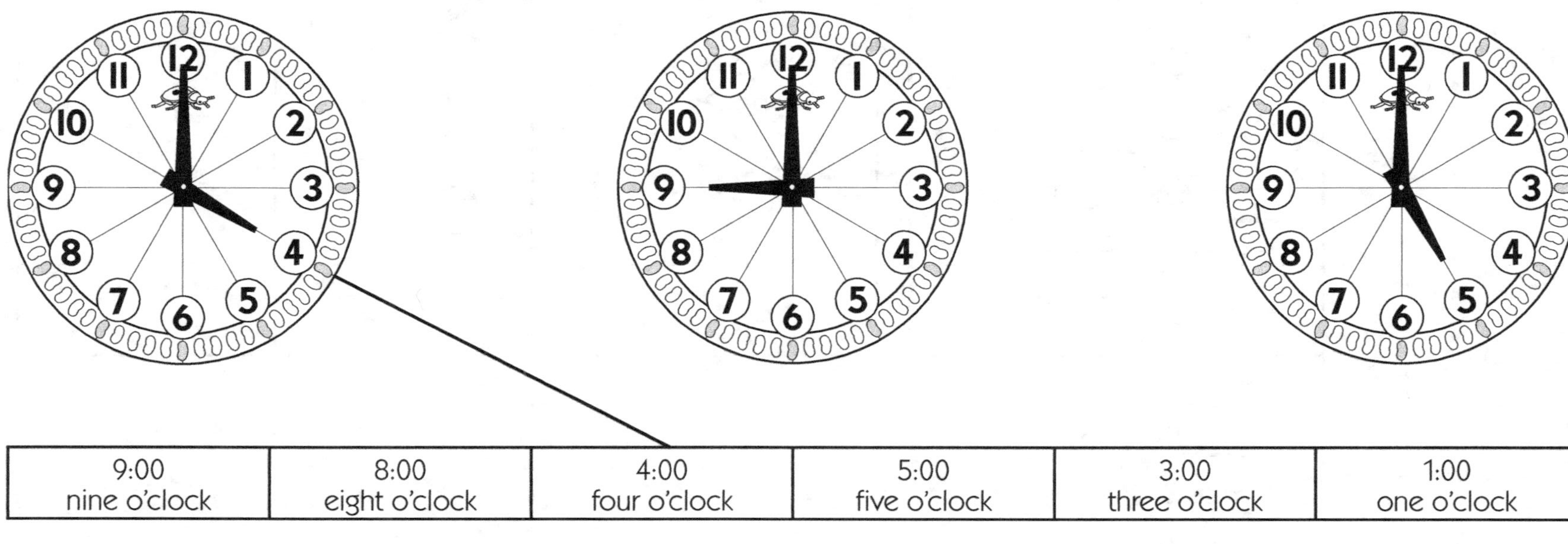

| | | | | | |
|---|---|---|---|---|---|
| 9:00<br>nine o'clock | 8:00<br>eight o'clock | 4:00<br>four o'clock | 5:00<br>five o'clock | 3:00<br>three o'clock | 1:00<br>one o'clock |

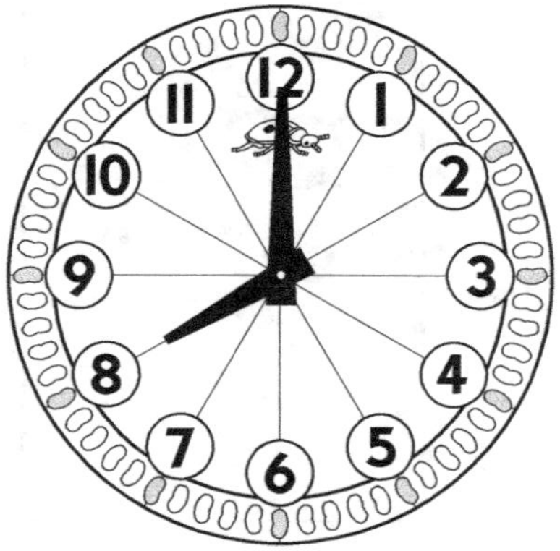

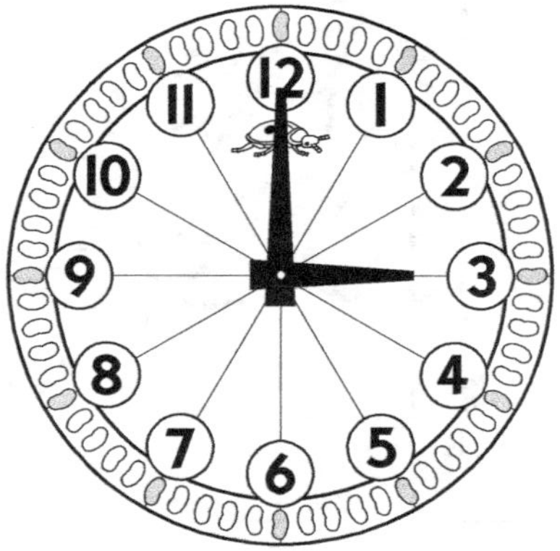

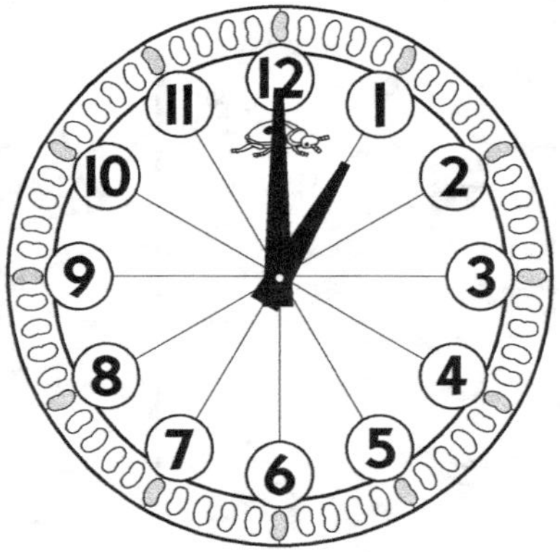

# More about 4

Trace the numbers. Fill in the missing numbers to complete the equations. Use the pictures to help.

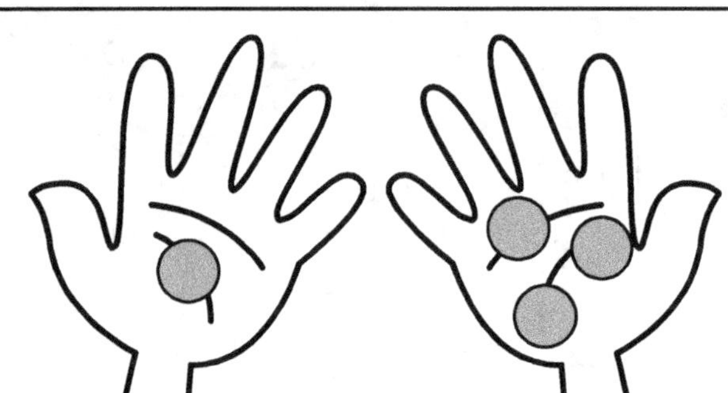

___ + ___ = 4

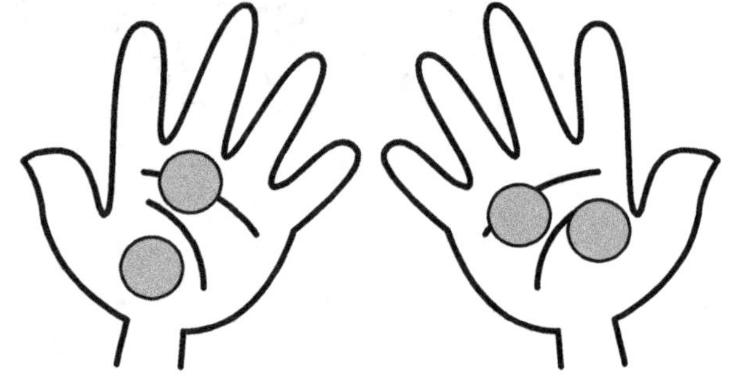

___ + ___ = 4

3 + ___ = 4

2 + ___ = 4

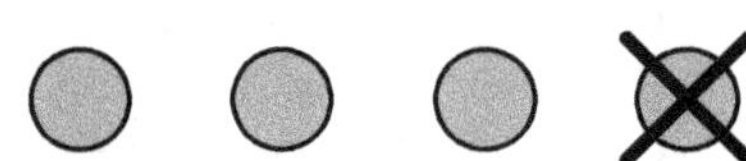

4 − 1 = 3

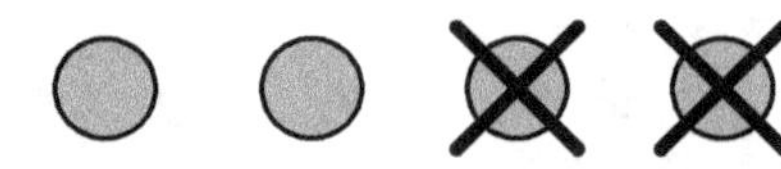

4 − 2 = 2

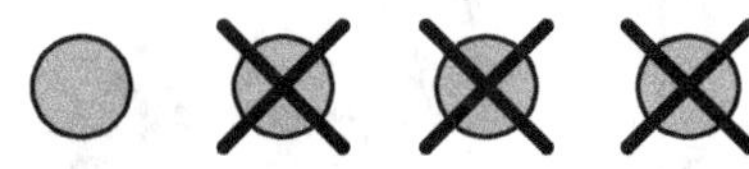

4 − 3 = 1

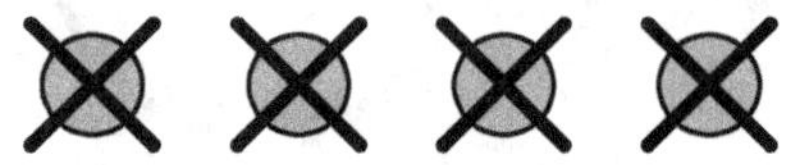

4 − 4 = 0

# What's Missing? Sheet 3

Fill in the missing numbers. Use the pictures to help.

_______¢ + 3¢ = 5¢

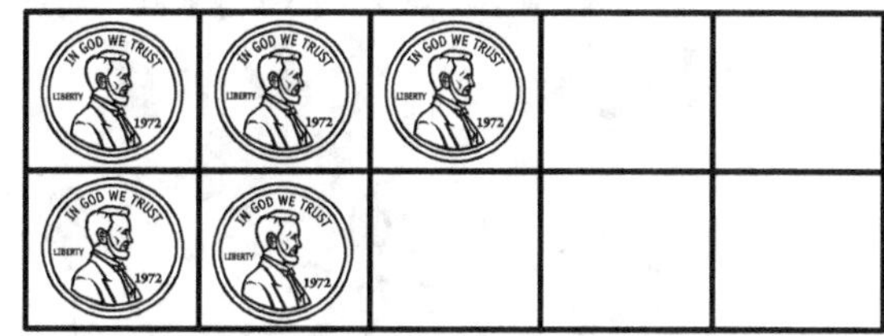

_______¢ + 2¢ = 5¢

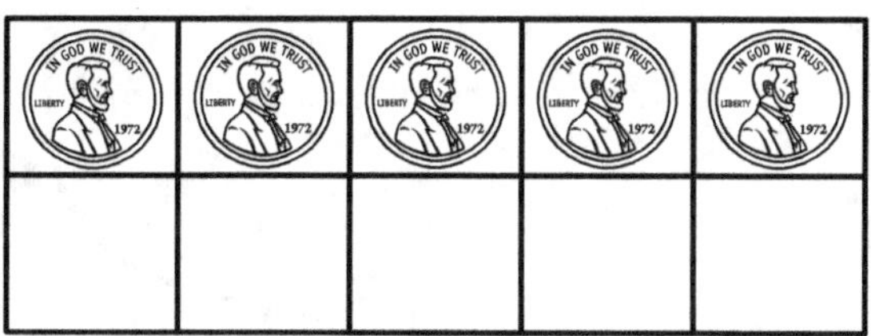

_______¢ + 0¢ = 5¢

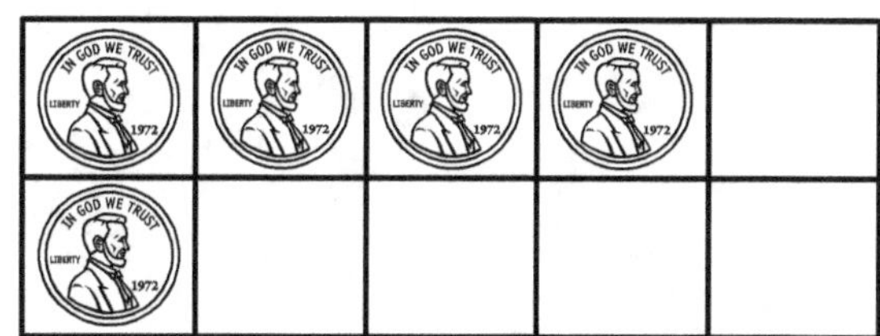

_______¢ + 1¢ = 5¢

_______¢ + 4¢ = 5¢

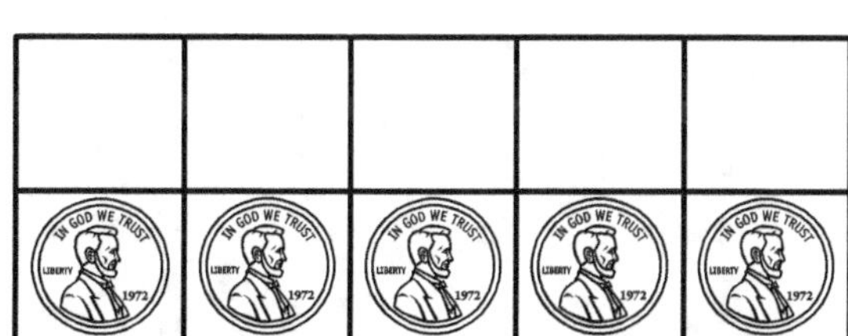

_______¢ + 5¢ = 5¢

## Frog Story Problem

Use pictures and numbers to show how you solve the problem.

## More Frog Problems

Use pictures and numbers to show how you solve each problem.

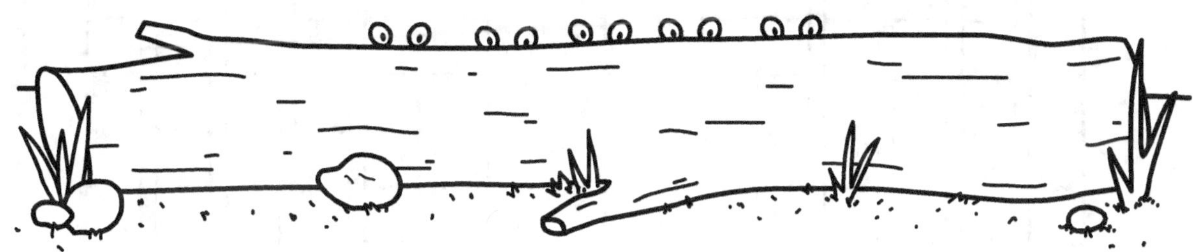

# Counting By Fives  Sheet 1

**1** Trace each number.

5   10   15   20   25   30

**2** How many cubes in each set? Write the numbers.

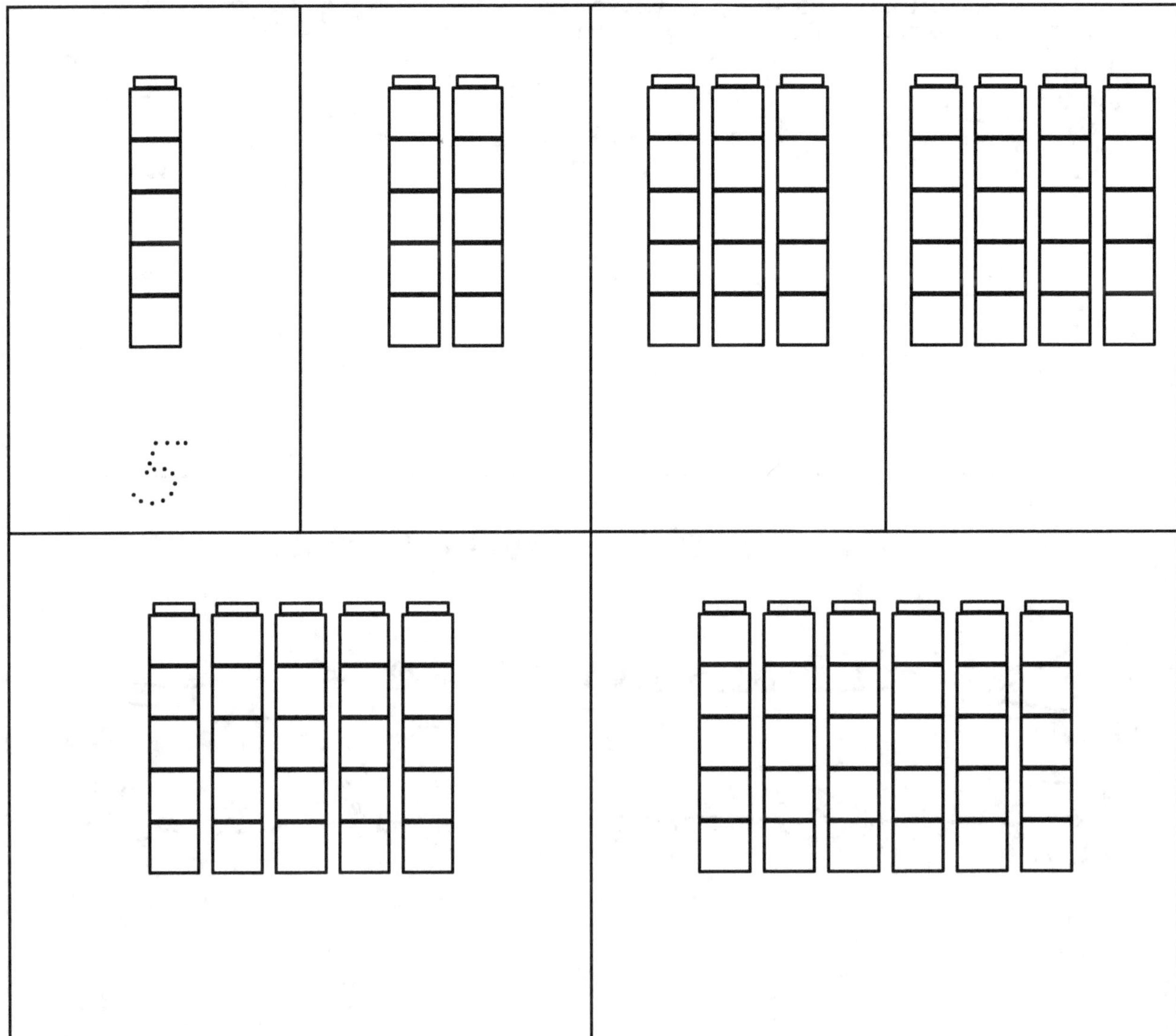

# Counting Nickels

Use the following information to help solve the problems below.

     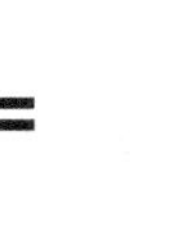 

5¢
1 nickel

**1** Trace each number.

5  10  15  20  25  30

**2** How many cents? Write the amount.

   _____ ¢

   _____ ¢

    _____ ¢

     _____ ¢

      _____ ¢

# More about 5

Trace the numbers. Fill in the missing numbers to complete the equations.

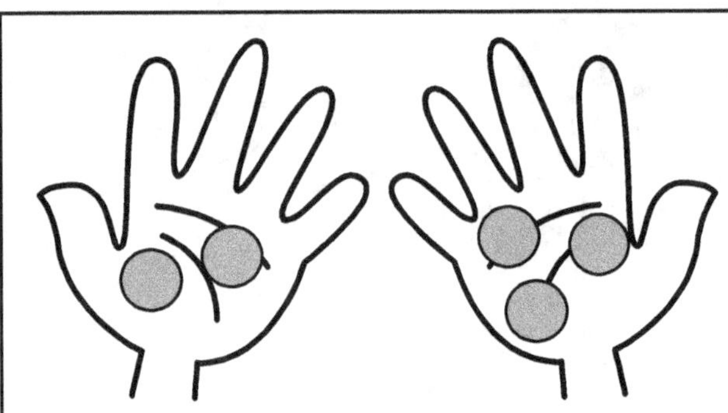

___ + ___ = 5

___ + ___ = 5

3 + ___ = 5

2 + ___ = 5

5 − 1 = 4

5 − 2 = 3

5 − 3 = 2

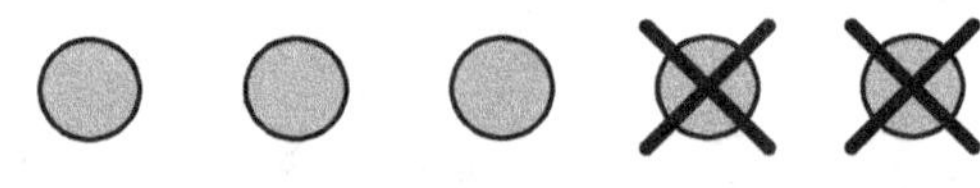

5 − 4 = 1

NAME ______________________ DATE ____________

# Counting By Fives Sheet 2

**1** Trace each number.

5 10 15 20 25

30 35 40 45 50

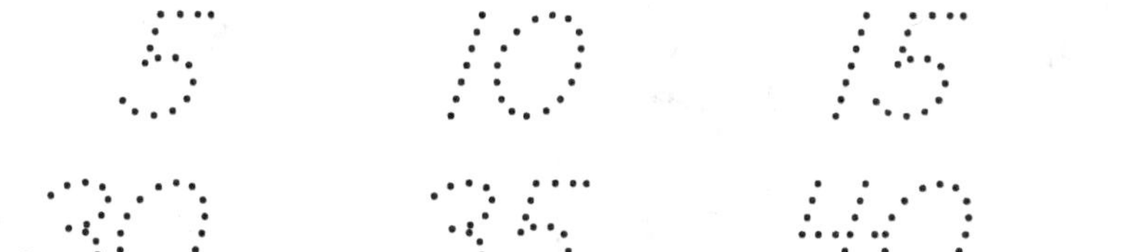

**2** How many cubes in each set? Write the numbers.

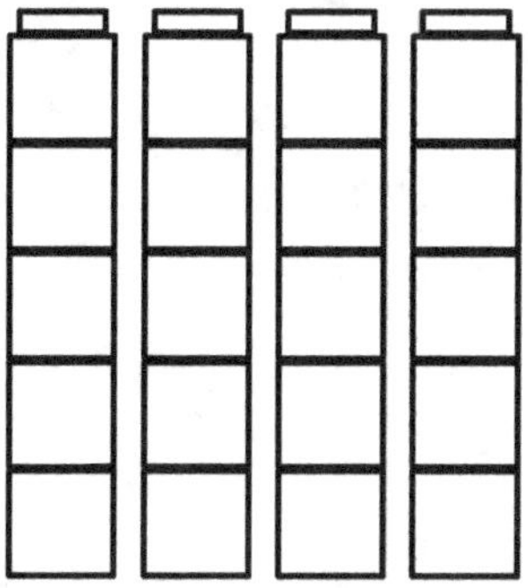

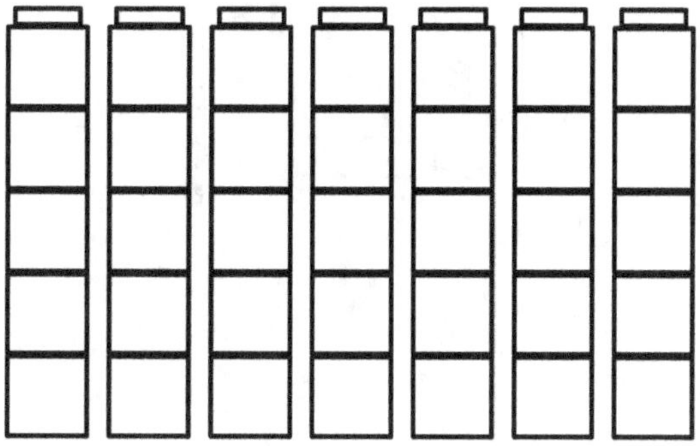

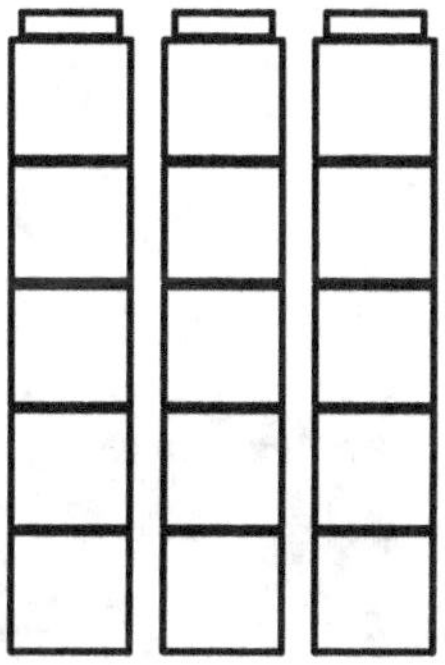

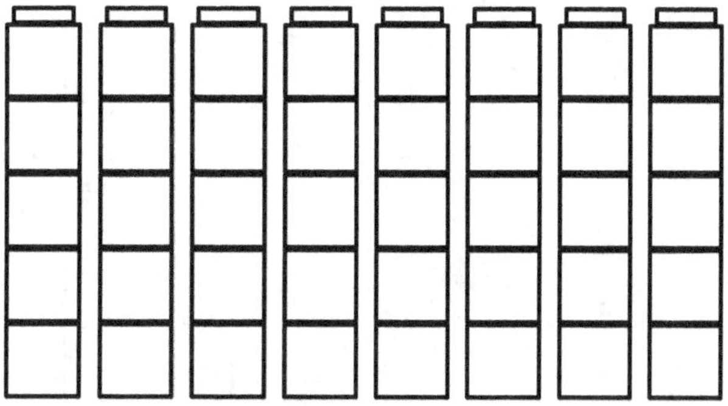

## Morning or Evening?

Draw lines to connect the pictures to morning or evening.

Morning

Evening

# More about 6

Trace the numbers. Fill in the missing numbers to complete the equations.

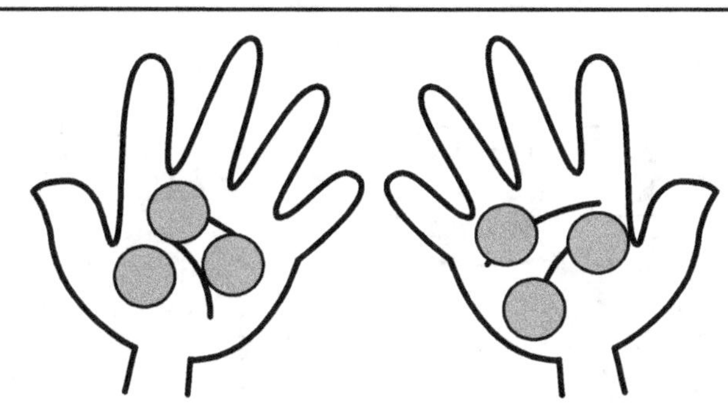

___ + ___ = 6

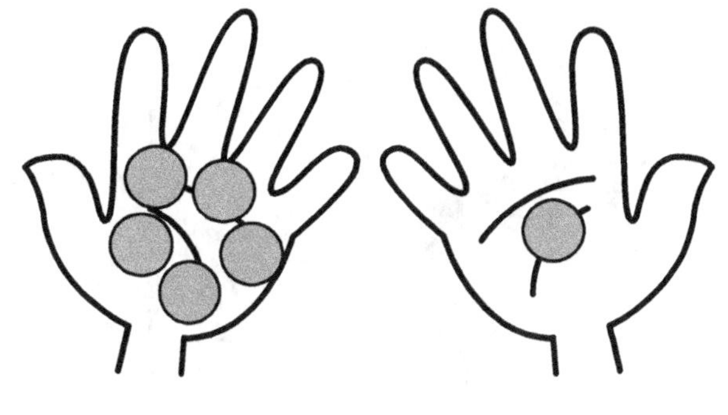

___ + ___ = 6

4 + ___ = 6

2 + ___ = 6

6 − 1 = 5

6 − 2 = 4

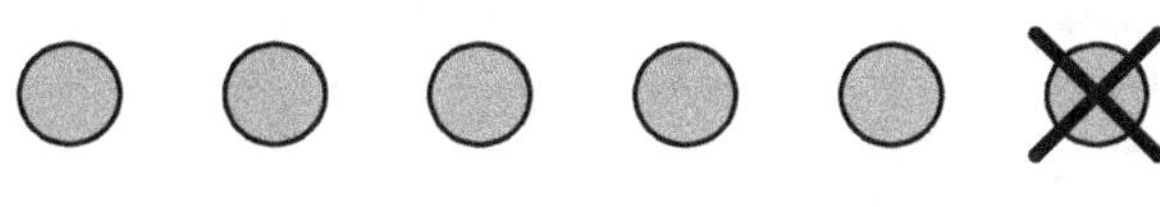
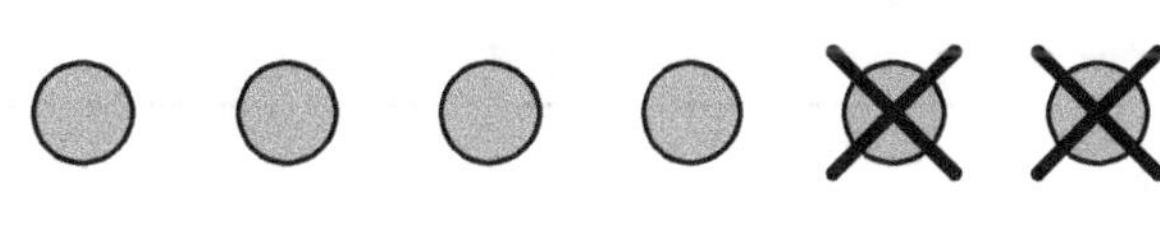

6 − 3 = 3

6 − 4 = 2

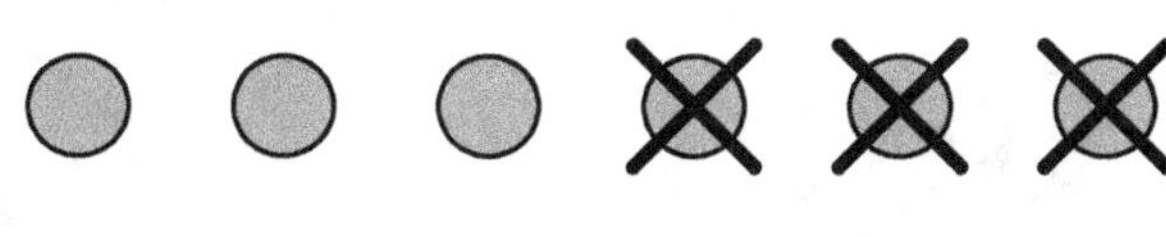
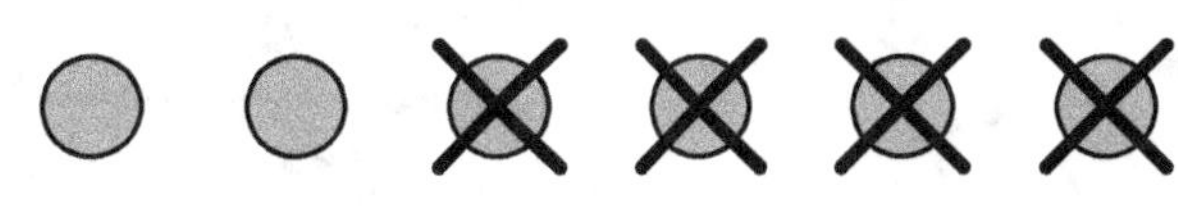

# More or Less Time?

Circle the picture in each box that would take you *more* time.

# The Frog Jumping Contest

**1** Freddy Frog is practicing for the big frog jump contest. Color in the boxes to show how far he jumped each time.

1st Jump: 8 sticks

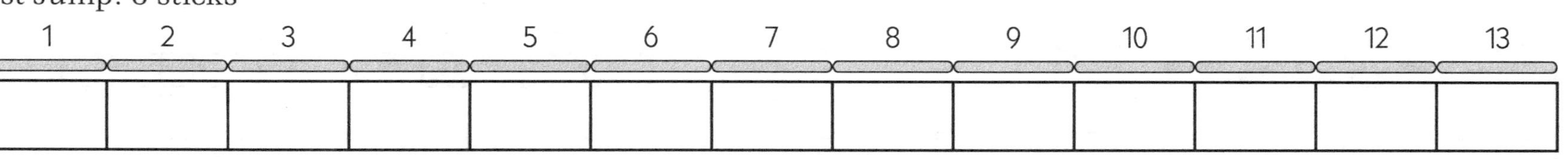

2nd Jump: 12 sticks

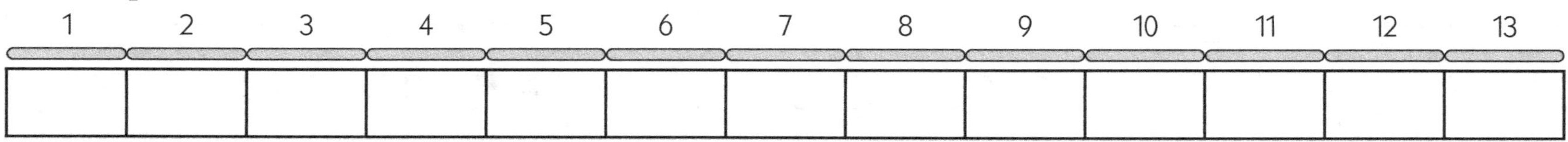

3rd Jump: 9 sticks

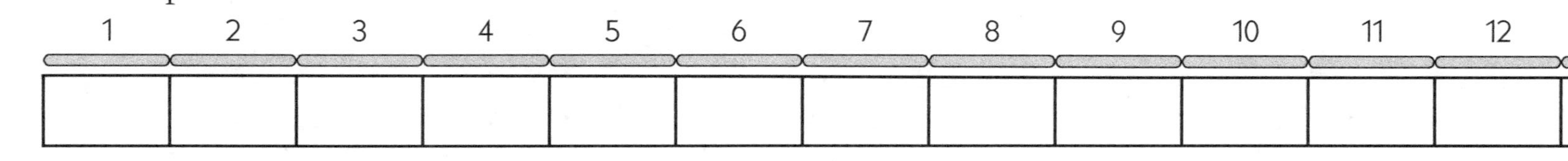

**2** Which one was his longest jump? (Circle one.)  1st  2nd  3rd

**3** Which one was his shortest jump? (Circle one.)  1st  2nd  3rd

# Counting By Tens

**1** Trace each number.

10  20  30  40  50  60  70  80

**2** How many cubes?

| | |
|---|---|
|  | 30 |
|  | |
|  | |
|  | |

# Frog Addition

**1** Color the frogs. Trace the numbers or symbols. Write an addition sentence to match the picture.

Color 2 frogs green. Color 3 frogs brown.

$2 + 3 = $ ______

Color 4 frogs red. Color 1 frog blue.

______ $+$ ______ $=$ ______

Color 3 frogs yellow. Color 2 frogs black.

______ $+$ ______ $=$ ______

**2** Add.

$$\begin{array}{cccccc}
1 & 3 & 4 & 2 & 3 & 4 \\
+\,2 & +\,1 & +\,1 & +\,2 & +\,2 & +\,2 \\
\hline
\end{array}$$

# Frog Line-Up

**1** The frogs are lined up for the big race! Color the frogs so it's easy to tell them apart.

- Color the 1st frog green.
- Color the 4th frog brown.
- Color the 2nd frog yellow.
- Color the 5th frog red.
- Color the 3rd frog blue.
- Color the 6th frog black.

**2** Here is the race track. Fill in the missing numbers.

| 1 |  | 3 |  | 5 |  | 7 |  | 9 |  |
|---|---|---|---|---|---|---|---|---|---|

**3** Color in the boxes on the track.

- Color the 1st box red.
- Color the 6th box blue.
- Color the 2nd box green.
- Color the 7th box red.
- Color the 3rd box blue.
- Color the 8th box green.
- Color the 4th box red.
- Color the 9th box blue.
- Color the 5th box green.

**4** What color should the 10th box be? ______________________________ Color it in!

**5** Add.

$$
\begin{array}{ccccccc}
0 & 0 & 1 & 2 & 2 & 2 & 3 \\
+\,0 & +\,1 & +\,1 & +\,1 & +\,2 & +\,3 & +\,3 \\
\hline
\end{array}
$$

# Frog Subtraction

**1** Color the frogs. Trace the numbers or symbols. Write a subtraction sentence to match the picture.

Color 4 frogs green. Cross out 2 of them.

4 − 2 = _______

Color 5 frogs red. Cross out 1 of them.

5 − 1 = _______

Color 6 frogs brown. Cross out 3 of them.

_______ − _______ = _______

**2** Subtract.

| 2 | 3 | 4 | 5 | 5 | 6 | 6 |
|---|---|---|---|---|---|---|
| − 1 | − 2 | − 2 | − 3 | − 4 | − 1 | − 2 |

# Match the Shapes

Draw lines to match the shapes.

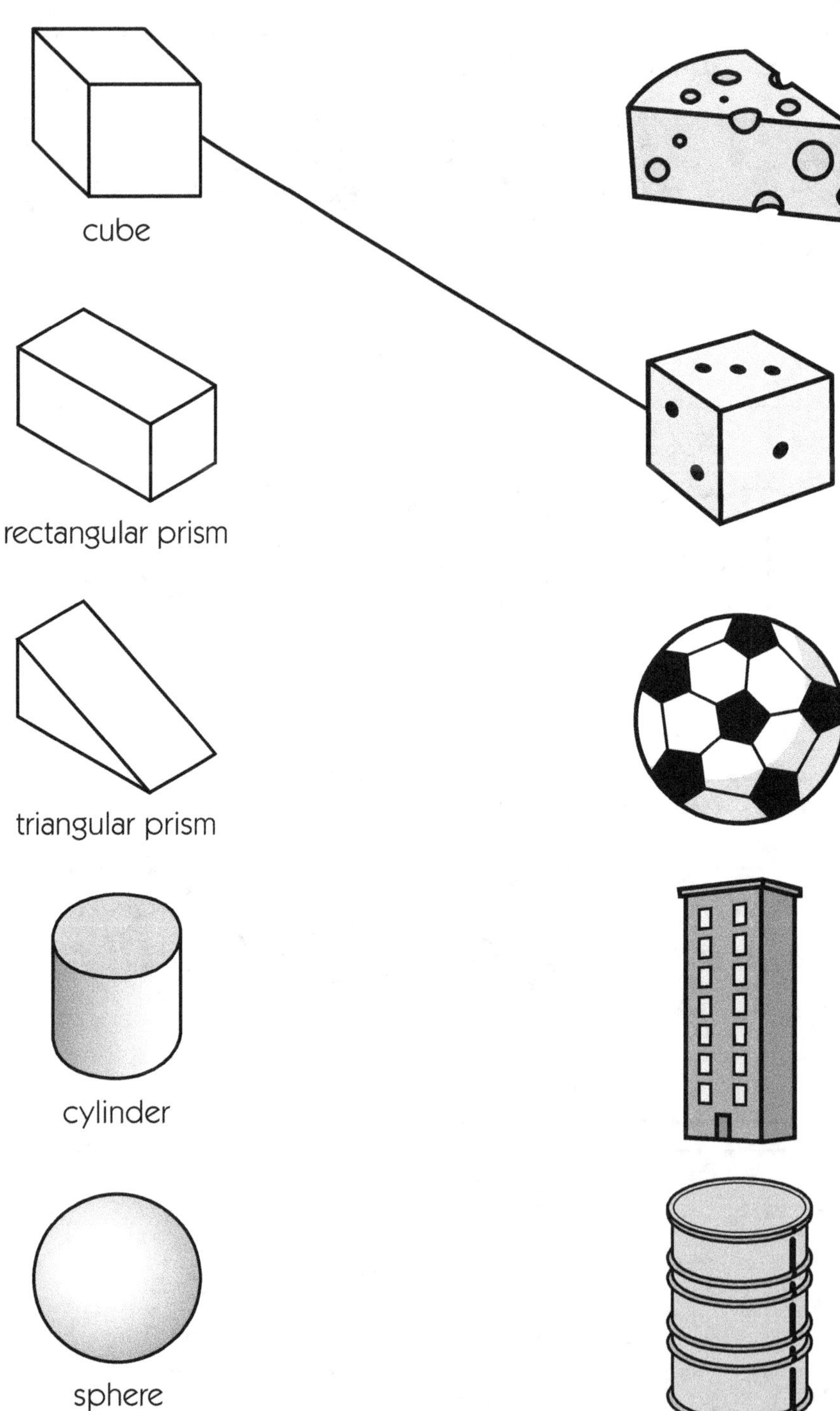